FIRED WITH ENTHUSIASM

FIRED WITH ENTHUSIASM

*A Take-Charge Game Plan for
a Quick Career Comeback*

TOM LONERGAN

**Andrews McMeel
Publishing**

Kansas City

Fired with Enthusiasm copyright © 1998 by Tom Lonergan. All rights reserved. Printed in the United States of America. No part of this book may be used or reproduced in any manner whatsoever without written permission except in the case of reprints in the context of reviews. For information, write Andrews McMeel Publishing, an Andrews McMeel Universal company, 4520 Main Street, Kansas City, Missouri 64111.

www.andrewsmcmeel.com

98 99 00 01 02 EBI 10 9 8 7 6 5 4 3 2 1

Library of Congress Cataloging-in-Publication Data

Lonergan, Tom.
   Fired with enthusiasm / Tom Lonergan.
      p. cm.
   ISBN 0-8362-5210-1 (pbk.)
   1. Career changes.   2. Vocational guidance.   3. Employees—Dismissal of.   I. Title.
HF5384.L66   1998
650. 14—dc21   97-40511
                                                                                                          CIP

ATTENTION: SCHOOLS AND BUSINESSES

Andrews McMeel books are available at quantity discounts with bulk purchase for educational, business, or sales promotional use. For information, please write to: Special Sales Department, Andrews McMeel Publishing, 4520 Main Street, Kansas City, Missouri 64111.

· Contents ·

Introduction

vii

I. Just Stay in the Game

3

II. Why Were You Fired?

9

III. Why Does It Hurt?

29

CONTENTS

IV. Sex and Expectations

43

V. How to Make It All Work

61

VI. What to Look for in Them

89

VII. Starting Up

101

VIII. Marathons and Long Walks

123

IX. The Jerks You Leave Behind

139

X. The End?

149

XI. Pay Attention to These

151

· Introduction ·

Fired? Wish you were? Or just worried you might be? This is the book for you. Misfit, renegade, any poor slob caught in the office meat grinder, this book will show you how to pick yourself up and turn your life around. I know because I've been there myself. I'm not a career consultant, outplacement advisor, or human resources drone. I'm a victim, just like you. I've been a president. CEO. Company founder. Yet I've been fired more times than a Smith & Wesson.

I know how you feel. And I'm not going to waste your time with some sophomoric tutorial on interview skills or how to prepare a résumé. The last time I was out of a job, I picked up the two leading no-nonsense books on the market. Written by career management gurus. People who make their living handing out advice. You know what they told me? The opening line of one was "Times are tough," and the opening line of the second was "Layoffs aren't going away." Big news!

This book is about changing your life. Right now. Rebalancing the scales in your favor. And there's not a thing this book recommends that you can't do for yourself today, whether you still have a job or just lost one. I'm going to give you some real perspective, some positive action to take to turn things around for yourself. I'm going to tell you real war stories, and I'm going to make you laugh. Because next to a stiff Jack Daniels, laughter is sometimes the best friend you've got.

First a little story about class. Back in the sixties, Clark Kerr, the president of the University of California at Berkeley, got fired for doing his job. He'd failed to crack down on the student free-speech movement, the baptismal sixties protest. He'd held back, refused to call in the police against a paralyzing campuswide protest. Instead, he let the students' little drama play itself out without incident or injury.

Years before the time when decisions by reactionary administrators at other schools would result in the use of tear gas and violence, Kerr had refrained. And for that he lost his job. Governor Ronald Reagan pressured the California Board of Regents to fire Kerr in 1967. It was a bum rap. Kerr got the boot while the student protesters got to stay.

I was a student at the time myself, sympathetic to

the issues of the free speechers. And I couldn't help feeling sorry for the guy. Hell, he'd done nothing worse than keep a cool head in very uncool times. On the day he left his job, he faced the music smiling. He stood before a cheering crowd of supporters, punched his fist in the air and shouted, "Today I leave this job the way I started it: Fired with enthusiasm!"

Enthusiasm! Why not? Why not stand tall and grin right back in the face of bad news? These are questions I've had to ask myself a lot lately. In the past ten years, I've been fired four times. Twice from start-up companies I founded myself. Once from a company I spent four long years turning around. Once from my twenty-three–year marriage.

In the spring of 1996, I was riding high. House in the suburbs. Wife. Kids. I was at the top of a very successful software company. Happy and secure. But in less than nine months, it was all gone. My wife left me. I lost the house, my car. And on New Year's Day, 1997, my partners ganged up on me and fired me from my own company.

I'd just closed the largest deal in the company's history. Helped conceive the company's product line. Brought in more business in one year than everyone else on the staff, combined. I was a founder. Major stockholder. But I was tossed out like dryer lint because some enlightened investor decided it was time to "retool" the team.

FIRED WITH ENTHUSIASM

The team. I guess I know how it feels to be cut from the team. You feel like a leper. Afraid to face your friends and neighbors. Even your own family. Why is that? It's because you've just been humiliated in the most public and hurtful way possible. Rejected and shamed by someone you know in your heart is dumber than a plant.

Business just isn't nice anymore. Not like it was. That's why those self-help books just don't cut it. The people who write them have never been there themselves. Not like us. They may see it happen all the time—firings and layoffs. But it's always to someone else. They remain secure in their jobs and can't possibly understand the hurt, the guilt, the panic in the middle of the night. At a party. At your kid's soccer game.

Remember when business was like Harvard University? Harvard's admissions policy used to say that once you're in, you stay in. If you've been admitted as a freshman, you're pretty much assured of graduating. The school makes that commitment to you. When was the last time an employer made a commitment to you?

I went to a more enlightened university. The day I started school, the dean assembled the entire class in an auditorium and instructed us to look at the person on our left and the person on our right. We were all nervous as hell. We smiled thinly at one another and then quickly looked away. "Only one of the three of you will graduate." That was the only commitment the dean would make. One out of three. He was right, too. I made it. The other two didn't. And I've been looking to my left and right ever since.

It's a cold and graceless world. Things are changing all around us. Fast. And the clowns at the controls don't have a clue what to do next. They hack and slash. But who can blame them? They're all on the verge of being hacked and slashed themselves. Take the guy at the top, the one who fired you and me. He'll die by his own sword soon enough. You can count on it. The life expectancy for the average big shot is measured in heartbeats, not years.

Don't let the other ducks nibble at your tail. Remember that advice to the ugly duckling? Well, you know what? We're not the ugly ducklings they told us about at the office. We're swans. And just because the people at the top have no room for us on their org chart, it doesn't change a thing. We have value and worth. It's time to spread our wings and reinvent ourselves. Declare victory. Move on to new ponds.

Fired with Enthusiasm

I.

Just Stay in the Game

(Job Search Journal)
January 6

I just got fired on Friday afternoon. Four years on the job, and now I'm out in the street. What an awful weekend! I took my sons to the football game on Sunday. It was the NFL playoffs, and sixty thousand people were in the stands. A very big day. Yet all I kept thinking was that all those people around me had jobs and I didn't.

So it's Monday morning. You wake up, heart pounding in your chest like a bell ringing in an empty church. Your stomach is churning. And panic hits like a truck.

Welcome to life on the bottom rung.

You try to roll over, bury yourself under the covers. What difference does it make if you get up? You have nowhere to go, nothing to do. But just try sleeping in. You can't.

So get up. Get dressed and grab that coffee. Turn the chair toward the window and watch the sunrise, the snow fall, the rain. Life goes on. As of today, man has put in 2.5 million years on this planet. Congratulations. You've just helped add to the unbroken string.

"Sometimes you're winning if you just stay in the game."

Marvin Mitchelson, the divorce lawyer, said that to me at a craps table in the Bahamas. It was 1981, and I'd just left my first real job to start my first company. I had a wife and two small kids. I'd mortgaged my house to the hilt and had a Small Business Administration loan that was nearly ten times what my previous annual salary had been.

Stay in the game? How was I supposed to do that?

Mitchelson and I stood next to each other at the bumper of the crap table that night, chummy as kids. He slapped me on the back, and I kept rolling winners. But we were on opposite sides of life's calculus that night. He was in Nassau contesting what was then the largest divorce settlement ever. Two and a half billion dollars for a twenty-something oil sheik's wife. And I was in Nassau because I'd just extended my credit cards to their limit. I'd taken a trip I shouldn't have taken because winter back home was wearing me out. I took a big risk, and I was very glad I did because that night I managed to win enough money to pay for the entire trip. I took a gamble getting into the game. And I've managed to stay in the game ever since.

Sometimes you're winning if you just stay in the game.

I read a front-page story in the *Wall Street Journal* about a ninety-eight-year-old woman who's getting a full-court press from Hollywood for a book she self-published nearly twenty years ago. The bidding started at $375,000 and ballooned quickly to $1 million. Using true poetic license, the *Journal* called Jesse Lee Brown Foveaux of Manhattan, Kansas, an "overnight sensation."

Overnight?

Mrs. Foveaux defines resilience. When she was eighty, she wrote in longhand her memoirs of a hardscrabble life: marriage, divorce, alcoholism. She published the first editions of her book herself. For years, she walked the streets of Manhattan, Kansas, handing out copies to people who'd heard about the book from others.

What is it about us that enables us to persevere? What sustains an unpublished writer through ninety-eight years? What enables an Olympic runner to get back in the race after he's fallen down? What keeps a soldier marching back into combat? And how come some people can do it and others can't?

Character.

A wise friend once told me that character is not like a statue. Once you build it, it doesn't stand for all time.

FIRED WITH ENTHUSIASM

Character has to be worked on every damned day. Some people make up their minds to the effort. Others don't.

During the Dark Ages, Attila the Hun torched all of Europe. Then, for some reason, at the gates of Paris he stopped. He pitched his tents and he waited. Finally, a fourteen-year-old girl named Genevieve left the city by herself and went out to Attila's encampment. What she did there, what she said, remains a mystery. But by the time she returned to the city, Attila had packed up his tents and horsemen and ridden off, sparing Paris.

Today St. Genevieve is the patron saint of Paris, a city that no invading army since Attila has attempted to disturb. Even the Nazis chose to enter the city peacefully during their conquest of France in World War II.

Character has won more wars than emperors and generals. In 400 B.C., a handful of Spartans at Thermopylae kept more than 100,000 Persians from destroying ancient Greece. In 1863, a school teacher from Maine saved the Battle of Gettysburg for the Union army. And in 1944, a series of individual acts of heroism kept D-Day from becoming a cruel disaster.

Resilience. Character. And just making a start.

Winston Churchill once said that 90 percent of success is just showing up. Just getting out of bed and making a start.

Starts don't need to be perfect. Most writers end up throwing out the first few pages of any new effort. The same is true of painters. It takes time to work into a subject, to find the right voice, the right colors and texture. Sometimes you need to write four pages to finally get one good paragraph. To fill two or three canvases in order to get one good image. That's because the human mind is self-lubricating. It grows more efficient by exercise.

Resilience. Character. Making a start. This is life's calculus. But it's hard to read about resilience when you're flat on your back. It's hard to think about character or even making a new start when you're down and out.

Some days there are just too many questions. How did this happen, and why does it hurt? I want to push myself back up to my feet, but I need to know what to do next. How long is it going to take to reach the next mark? How much effort is it going to take to get where I need to be? And where will the energy and help come from?

That's what this book is for. To examine these questions. To find answers. So we can stay in the game, sustain the effort and, sometimes, if we have to, make a new start.

II.

Why Were You Fired?

January 10

Why me? What am I going to do now? I can't even go out of the house, can't face my family or friends. I feel lost, abandoned, ashamed.

Fired. Where does the word come from? A bad pun on the word *discharge*. To *discharge* a weapon. *Fire* a pistol.

But why does it happen? Lots of reasons. And most of them have nothing to do with you. Get used to that. It's probably not your fault. Probably it was someone else's. Some fool with the wrong agenda. But what does it matter now? Today's a new day. Time to start fresh.

Remember when the most important thing in life was your grades? You'd kill for good grades, right? Yet how many people since college have ever asked you what your grades were? None. And five years from now, do you think anyone will remember you were fired from your job today? Do you think anyone will care?

· People Screw Up ·

Remember the tale about the emperor with no clothes? Naked in front of the whole world? Yet his subjects didn't have the courage to tell him so. In fact, everyone made up the most absurd fantasies about his robes and trousers, jackets and shoes. Anything to keep the emperor happy.

I know another good emperor story. Taken from Chinese proverbs. It's the story of the emperor's horses. How the emperor sent a man to find the finest horses in the land. How the man searched for months, and when he finally returned, he was nearly put to death because he couldn't remember what color the horses were he'd just brought back.

The man had chosen horses for the emperor based on their inner qualities. Spirit, stamina, and grace. Qualities unrecognized by emperors and lesser men. The man was so good at seeing these qualities, so good at keeping all distractions from his eye, he never noticed less important attributes, like color. For this, the emperor thought him a fool.

We all know emperors. Ones who think they're dressed

when they're not. Ones who think they know all about horses and who don't want anyone telling them otherwise. Sure, emperors have power. They can make us pack up our stuff. Make us hang our heads and clear out. But they can never take away what we know about horses. Remember that.

Don't let emperors affect the way you think. The temptation is to take the criticisms of your old bosses too seriously. While it's good to learn from past mistakes, it can be paralyzing to focus too much on them now.

How do you strike a good balance? I'll tell you a good trick. Take a piece of blank paper and write down all the things you were told you did wrong on your last job. Take your time. Don't rush through it. When you're finished, read through the list once. Then burn it.

Now you've accomplished the two most important steps necessary for moving on. You've given careful consideration to past mistakes. And you've pushed them out of your mind. That's two very big steps forward.

· They Never Remember Your Victories ·

Billy Martin managed the Yankees on and off for at least a dozen years. He was fired three times by George Steinbrenner. Hired back, then fired again. Each time, he'd build the team and win a championship. But once he started to lose, good-bye. Then without him, the

FIRED WITH ENTHUSIASM

team would fall from the top like a brick, and he'd be hired back again.

Peaks and valleys. That's what Billy Martin called his life. Every time he was up, he got knocked down. We all live like that. One defeat away from the door. One paycheck from unemployment. It's "what have you done for me lately" and "see ya."

You close a big deal today, and by tomorrow all anyone wants to know is when you're going to close another. You run like hell and have a big quarter, or a big year, and it's on to the next.

Zero-based management. That's what it is. No credit for past victories. Just debits and pink slips for losses. It's worse than prison. Employers keep you on a treadmill until you fall down or get knocked off. And they give you no damned compensation for good behavior.

Now it's up to you to sell yourself. Write your victories down on paper. All of them, so you don't forget. Successful projects. Big sales. Don't embellish. But don't leave any out. When you're done, use them as the basis to build your résumé. That's what it's there for. To focus you and anyone you talk to on the successes your previous employer chose to ignore. Make them the foundation of your future plans.

Remember, a résumé is nothing more than your name, address, and telephone number, and some collateral information that makes your name, address, and telephone number memorable. It's like when you were dating. The things you said on a first date that made someone want to remember to call you. You bragged. You picked the things you'd done in your life that you were proudest of, and you talked them up.

The same is true with your victories. Brag about them. Get them down on paper. Build your résumé around them so that someone will remember your name, address, and telephone number. But try to keep it to one page.

· You Never Learned to Play the Game ·

I'm no rocket scientist. I studied quantum physics for half a semester and ended up talking to myself. Instead, I was trained in operations research. Trained to build organizations and teams, to make them run more efficiently and smoothly.

At college, I remember learning one thing above all. The goal of a good manager is to work himself out of a job. Do things efficiently. Improve. Delegate. A corollary to this rule is that a good manager knows he's doing his job when all he has to do each day is sit with his feet up on his desk and watch his department hum. Ever try doing that? You'd get fired in a minute, whether your department was humming or not.

Albert Einstein was once asked what he would do if he had eight minutes to defuse a bomb. His answer?

FIRED WITH ENTHUSIASM

He'd spend the first seven minutes just thinking about it, only one minute defusing the bomb. Think that would work on your old job? Do nothing but think? Fat chance.

Our lives are run by people who think that to be effective you have to work seventy or eighty hours a week. Run like hell. Meetings. E-mail. Voice mail. Travel to the coast, Europe, Japan. The effort becomes more important than the result. And you get penalized if you don't play the game. But who wants to play that game? Making nothing to do look like having a lot to do?

You're finished with all that. For once you have no one to answer to but yourself. Take the time to make an efficient plan. Get everything down on paper. And be flexible. Be prepared to rip your plan up and make a new one, every day if necessary.

How do you start? I remember something I learned from my son when he was in elementary school. He taught me how to make happy/sad lists. You take a blank piece of paper. Down one side you write all the things that make you happy. On the other side, all the things that make you sad. It's like a balance sheet, and it's a great beginning to your plan.

Write down all the things you have going for you and all the things going against you. Try to match an item of one with an item of the other, and your plan will begin to take shape. I had an outplacement counselor recommend the same idea to me a few months later. It really works.

Remember also to set yourself some goals, some meetable goals. And reward yourself. Don't worry if you're working ten minutes or ten hours a day. That's for the people who don't know how to measure real achievement. Two or three hours a day is sufficient. You're in a world now where looking busy just isn't good enough.

Think back to your old job. How much time was wasted there? At least an hour every day trying to explain what you were doing to someone else. Well, that's no longer necessary now that there's just you. Also that hour listening to someone else try to explain to you what she was doing. No longer necessary.

An hour for reports. An hour for meetings. Add time for lunch and BS sessions in the coffee room, there's at least five or six hours of wasted office time you no longer have to spend. You work more efficiently now. More effectively. You have more time to think, to plan. Like Albert Einstein.

· A Conspiracy against Good Ideas ·

What will drive economic growth in the new millennium? Good old-fashioned hard work? Longer hours? More meetings? Wrong. This is the age of ideas. Creativity. Innovation. Companies like Intel, Microsoft, even remakes of boring old farts like Ma Bell have built their strategies around creative ideas. Smart people.

Remember what happened when someone brought up a good idea at your former company? What happened when you brought up a good idea? Did people stop admiring the emperor's new clothes long enough to notice? Clap you on the back? Throw their support behind you 100 percent? I don't think so.

Every good idea you ever had was tanked. Right? Or worse: stolen. Snapped up by someone else who got all the credit. Screwed it up royally so there was nothing left for you but more long hours and hard work. And that's the way they wanted it. A conspiracy against ideas.

Ideas should be important to you again, the only one who matters. Each morning you ought to get up and make a list of good ideas. Because it matters. To you. I know a guy who got fired from a twenty-five-year job in manufacturing. Two months later, he was reading an outdoor magazine and decided to start a company making kayaks. Now he sells kayaks all over the world, grossing millions of dollars a year. And he still has only four employees.

Be creative. Brainstorm. The future is your next idea. And all it takes is one good one. You know how to generate ideas? Read. Newspapers. Books. Magazines. My favorite source is the *Wall Street Journal*. Try it. Read it every day. Try to spot trends.

Pick the section that has most to do with your field. Technology. Marketing. Advertising. Publishing. Look for news about companies and people you know who interest you. Pick a time of day when you're fresh and alert. Read the words and let the ideas take hold. It won't happen right away, but it's a good practice to get started.

Talk to people. They're another good source. Pick up the telephone. Tell someone about an article you just read. I'm an entrepreneur, and I claim to have never had an original idea. But I know one when I hear one. Most people are like that. They can help you recognize good ideas and refine them. Pick up the telephone and call someone. Talk about your ideas. Listen to theirs. See how good it feels again.

· They Never Liked You Anyway ·

Translation: Since we never liked them, they must have felt the same way about us. Of course, every college kid knows this isn't true. Otherwise, his parents would have stopped making tuition payments long ago. You don't have to like someone to be liked by them.

Generally, managers don't bear malice toward the people they fire. It's the kidnapper/victim thing. There's a bond that develops. You may hate him. But chances are, he doesn't hate you. If he did, he never would have fired you to begin with. He wouldn't dare. It's the hated ones who always keep their jobs. Ever notice that? That's because no one dares to confront them. Hated people are tiptoed around while liked people get clobbered.

I remember an incident that occurred shortly after the failure of my first start-up. It was a hi-tech company. A typical rags-to-riches-to-rags story. And when the dust settled and I managed to find another job, I ran smack into one of my old directors. A venture capital guy who was so hurt by my first failure that I was sure he'd never speak to me again.

It was in New York. My company had failed in the spring, and now it was summer. We literally ran into each other at a street corner. He smiled, and I felt like disappearing into the sidewalk. I was eating a hot dog, dressed in jeans and a sweatshirt. He was wearing a three-piece suit.

He asked what I was doing. And I didn't have the guts to tell him the truth, that I'd taken a lower-paying job. So, I lied. I told him I was quitting hi-tech altogether and getting into real estate. What a joke. It was 1987, and the real estate market was about to crash. But he jumped at it. Said to keep him in mind, he'd like to invest. Said he'd always believed in me. He'd just lost faith in hi-tech.

People have very short attention spans. Remember "what have you done for me lately"? It works both ways. If you can do something today for the guy who fired you yesterday, he'll love you for it.

Starting today, everyone likes you—even the ones who don't. Make up your mind to it. This isn't high school. People don't hold grudges. If you can do something for someone, help them make money, believe me, they'll listen to you. All you have to do is figure out a way to tell them. Send them a letter, a proposal. Don't be shy. Former employers? Them, too. Chances are, if you can make them some money, they'll all listen.

Try consulting or temping. There are dozens of people I know who returned to consult or temp for the same companies that had just fired them. All they did was let the dust settle on their firing and then send their old company a proposal. A little part-time consulting. A well-defined project to save the company money. Opportunity talks, and most people forget. Just give them time.

The people who like you already? They will always help. The people who are ambivalent toward you will respond to flattery. Ask them their advice and tell them you've always valued their judgment. The people who hate you will respond if you figure out a surefire way to make them money. Try it. Wait a little while. Then go back and hit them up for a favor. It's a damned good way to get even.

· You Were Making No Progress ·

My sister's husband once told me he thought all jobs progress through three important stages. Each stage is a conjugation of the verb *to be screwed up*. I'm screwed up. They're screwed up. We're all screwed up.

In the first stage, when you're a new hire, nothing makes sense to you. You're in way over your head, and nothing seems to go right. Everyone seems to be swimming strong strokes while you wallow. You feel screwed up.

By the time you hit the second stage, you have it all figured out. Then it's everyone else who's screwed up. You're champing at the bit to turn this baby on its ear. But everyone else is holding you back. They're ignorant. Incompetent. Dragging their feet. Nothing gets done.

In the third stage, everyone's so screwed up that no one can seem to get it right anymore. Not you. Not them. You're all tripping over each other, making things worse rather than better. Now you've made real progress.

Today you're a company of one. Congratulations. You have one employee and one product. Yourself. If you make a mistake, don't panic. Just fix it and go on. There's no one to blame. No one to hide behind. And no one to blame *you*. It's a perfect world indeed.

So, eliminate screwups from your vocabulary. Consider alternatives. Resourcefulness is a good one. A mistake can lead to a fix. That's resourcefulness. If you make a mistake, leave it for a while. Overnight ought to be enough. Then take a fresh look in the morning. Don't run away from problems. That's what everyone else does. Make up your mind that every problem is solvable and that really thorny problems lead to lucrative consulting jobs.

Of course, the best way to fix mistakes is to avoid them altogether. That's what a good plan is for. Ever hear the story of the carpenter who started out making railroad ties and ended up making toothpicks? He didn't have a template. Everyone needs a template. Individuals. Large organizations. Otherwise they get quickly off course. The railroad ties get smaller and smaller until. . . .

Make a daily template. Weekly templates. Like a company has its business plan, or an athlete has his daily training log. Keep track of what you did and what you plan to do. Use a calendar. Fill it up with notes. Look at it every morning and take your bearings. Try to avoid screwups but be ready for them when they come along.

· Living Life Backward ·

My older sister just got married for the first time last year. A year before that, she adopted her second child as a single parent. She has graduate degrees from Cornell and Columbia. She's worked for more than fifteen years as a consultant in the health care industry. On the day of her wedding, she told me she felt like she was living life backward. First she had her career. Then she had her children. Finally, she got a husband. Why not?

The same is true of getting fired. More than anything else, it requires starting over. Going back to the beginning. Living life backward. You've had your career. Now you have nothing. You had your own secretary. Now you have to learn how to type a résumé yourself. You were on top of the world. Now you have to go back to the bottom rung.

Living life backward can be cool. You've just got to learn to look at the positive aspects. You have a chance now to do something significant, a complete makeover of yourself and your life. You can take a giant step away from the plodders and into the world of ideas. Dream instead of mope.

But dreaming requires reinventing yourself. And reinventing yourself sometimes requires a giant step back. How do you step back? It's not easy. Some people just won't do it. But everybody *can* do it. It's like giving up smoking. You have to believe, really believe, that it's best for you to do it and bad not to. Reinvention is the hallmark of our times.

I once read an interview with the man who ran Westinghouse. He was retiring as CEO after thirty-five years, one of the most powerful executives in the country. Yet when the reporter asked if he'd do anything different with his life, the executive said he wished he'd started a dry-cleaning company instead. That's where the real money was, he said. Owning your own business. Building equity and value for yourself, rather than for some anonymous shareholder.

The Westinghouse CEO never had the courage to do what he really wanted, to reinvent himself. And he always regretted it, despite his apparent success.

Reinvention leads to opportunity, if not wealth. Stay where you are and you get trapped under an opportunity ceiling. You're never a hero in your own backyard, so there's only so far you can go. But get away, get out from under that ceiling, and the world becomes your oyster. Dry cleaning, consulting, entrepreneurship. The world is full of possibilities for those who dare to live their lives backward.

· Your Knees Ache ·

This is a pet concern of mine. I'm an addicted jogger. Twenty-five years of five-mile days, and my knees are killing me. Every day in the office, I sat with my chair rocked back and my feet up on my desk. Even if my brilliant management methods didn't always have things running smoothly, I still had to elevate my knees. People stopped, stared, joked about my "laid back" style. But I had no choice. Did this lead to my firing?

Illness. Poor health. We all worry that we're one missed workday away from unemployment. The kids are sick and home from school. Your mother has open-heart surgery. And our enlightened employers think it's smart to increase the stress we feel anyway with a nasty look whenever something unexpected happens. Whenever we need a favor.

I knew a guy who worked four years for the same company. Never took a sick day. Rarely took vacations. If there was a blizzard, he was the first one in to unlock the offices. The last one to leave after all the panicked drivers raced to beat the snowplows. When his mother had surgery, he waited until after hours to go visit her in the hospital. When his kids were sick, his wife stayed home. Think this made a difference?

Four years. And the guy was fired. Didn't have his

heart in it, they told him. A lame excuse. They just should have admitted the truth. It's the nature of the business world and has nothing to do with aching knees, or anything else. So forget about all the time off, feet up on the desk, fights with the boss. It's counterproductive. Focus on tomorrow. That's where your future is.

Winston Churchill knew how to forget the past and focus on the future. The man who led the Allies to victory in World War II fought his way back from one of the nastiest failures in history. During World War I, Churchill headed the British Admiralty, Britain's equivalent of our Navy Department. He took the blame for the catastrophic decision that allowed the German fleet to escape destruction and seek sanctuary in the Dardanelles. The Dardanelles mistake forced Turkey to enter the war on the side of the Germans and cost tens of thousands of lives. Churchill was forced out of office in disgrace.

But Churchill was a survivor. And it was his incredible instincts for survival that ultimately led to the defeat of the Nazis thirty years later in World War II. He never gave up on himself, never allowed himself to dwell on past disgraces, no matter how costly they were.

· Lonely Valleys ·

You're a professional. You've worked your whole life. You may have fallen into a lonely little valley, but after crossing through, you'll be back at work again. Maybe you'll do something altogether new. Start a new company. Open a business. Maybe not. But you can't take any baggage with you if you want to climb that next peak.

Why were you fired? Sometimes, it just happens. No one is immune, and no one is to blame. Not you. Not them. Not your knees, your ideas, your heart. Not conspiracies or games. Not even the emperor's new clothes. The sooner you let go of all that garbage, the sooner you can get on with what you need to do.

Climb back out and don't be bitter. Don't look back. To paraphrase the great Satchel Paige, someone's back there behind you. And you want to make damned sure you can use him as a reference someday.

· Summary of Things to Do ·

- While it's good to learn from past mistakes, it can be paralyzing trying to focus too much on them now; take a piece of blank paper and write down all the things they said you did wrong at your old job; read through it once, then rip it up and throw it away.

- Assemble all your victories on your résumé: awards, successful projects, big sales; don't embellish, but don't leave any out; make them the foundation of all your future plans.

- Make a list of personal assets; skills, experience, key contacts; match the things you have going for you with the things going against you; now you have the beginnings of a valuable personal planning tool.

- Be proactive; set yourself some realistic goals; start with something simple and reward yourself; don't worry at the end of each day that you didn't do more.

- Stay current; pick a time of day when you're most alert and read the *Wall Street Journal* or the business section of your local newspaper; follow your industry and its major markets; try to spot ideas, trends, opportunities.

- Get a calendar; fill it up with notes; take your bearings from it every day; keep track of what you do and what you intend to do; look forward and back and make changes to it often.

III.

Why Does It Hurt?

January 14

Life stinks! No job. No prospects. I'm ashamed to go out. Ashamed to stay in. Even ashamed to pick up the telephone. How long is this going to last? And what happens when the money runs out? I have a mortgage and bills. I've got to do something. Fast. Before I end up living in a box.

There's an arrow sticking in your back, and you just can't reach it to pull it out. You twist and turn, but you can't get to it. The pain won't go away. It's intense and bitter. It colors everything. Well, that's what being fired is like. Surgery without anesthesia.

What to do? Sometimes it helps to understand the pain and where it comes from.

· Frustration ·

We are the most competitive species on Earth. And because of natural selection, we are descended from the most aggressive members of our species through all history. That's a lot of baggage. Did you know that scientists in Ethiopia just discovered a 2.5-million-year-old cache of stone tools? Two and a half million years of hitting one another over the head with stone hammers. That's a lot of aggressive behavior.

Being fired with enthusiasm is like taking a megaton slap in the teeth. It lights the fuse on some pretty primitive hurt. Two and a half million years of don't-take-no-for-an-answer clobbers us with the need to strike back. But we're stuck. We can't do a thing but take the humiliation. No scalps, stone tools. No AK-47s in the lobby of the post office. Not even an argument. Just clear your stuff out and scram. Now.

We may think we want revenge. But do we really? I once saw a foreman lay off a woman only to have the woman toss a rock through his windshield on her way out the door. It did neither of them any good. Afterward they both stood together and cried. She felt worse. He felt worse.

Focus on positive action. Like what? Try asking your old boss to help you out with the names of some people to assist you in your search. That's right, the guy who fired you. No hard feelings. Hell, he probably feels so guilty about what happened, he'd do anything to help. All you need are a couple of names. A couple of leads. You'll feel good. He'll feel good. You can always get even later.

Start by writing him a letter. Better yet, send a card. Something cheerful. Tell him you understand why he had to do what he did, even if you don't. Tell him you respect his judgment and appreciated the opportunity to work with him. Tell him that being let go has allowed you to see things in a new light. Lie if you have to.

After a few days, follow up the letter with a phone call. Leave a very simple voice message. You're wondering if there's anyone he might suggest you talk with. You're just looking for ideas and advice. Don't expect anything to happen right away. But call again in a week or so. Sooner or later, you just might stop being the person he fired and start being the person he'll want to help out, just to get you off his back.

And remember, if he gives you a name, an idea, call back and say thanks. No matter how hard it is to do. Tell him how it went. Ask him if he has any more good ideas like the last one. A simple thank-you will get you more attention than a brick through a window. Very few people bother to say thanks anymore. Try it. Hell, you may end up being friends for life.

· Change Is a Bitch ·

For a nomadic people, we tolerate change pretty damned poorly. Where does that come from?

Throughout history, societies have succeeded only when they stopped long enough to put down roots. Build cities. Establish cultures. Over time, we reinvented ourselves from the free-swinging dudes and dudettes of the savanna. We became civilized. Stable. Stressed. Too bad, too, because now a whiff of instability hits us like a bad case of chicken pox. We get to itching and scratching until we finally settle into something new.

Change is good. Seasons. Leaves. Football coaches. Everything changes. Embrace change. It keeps us from going crazy. Remember, no job is forever. Even your old boss who fired you will be gone soon himself. You're the lucky one. You have the advantage. You're already out there, hustling, learning, making contacts. Just watch. You'll be the one he'll come to when it's his turn to be fired with enthusiasm.

But how do you learn to tolerate change? Practice. Start out with a few easy things. Go home and rearrange the furniture in your house. Buy a new outfit. Wear blue jeans instead of a suit. Take up jogging. Teach yourself some new tricks. Learn snowboarding or ballroom dancing. Whatever it takes to give yourself a little kick, a little change in perspective. After a while, you become more comfortable with change. And even more important, you become more comfortable with yourself. That's a very big step toward the self-reliance you'll need to turn things around for yourself.

I know a little bit about change myself. I've gone through more changes than Christianity. In the past twenty-five years, I've worked as a college coach and an engineer; founded my own computer-hardware company, computer-software company, and computer-services company; run a real-estate appraisal company; written; lectured; and gotten a carpenter's license. It can be done. No matter how old you are, you can always learn a new trick. Remember, Ray Kroc was retired and pushing sixty when he founded McDonald's. Stay flexible.

· Shut Out from the Herd ·

Firing cuts to the issue of rejection. We don't want to be alone, because life teaches some hard lessons to the loner. Separate yourself from the group, fall by the wayside, and you perish. That's what evolution has taught us.

But what do you really need to survive? Some good contacts. A telephone. Fax machine. Computer. Face it. It's never been easier to convert your kitchen into a

FIRED WITH ENTHUSIASM

virtual window on the world. Send a few letters. Maybe a fax. Pick up the telephone. Surf the Web. Except for groceries, you've got it all. Right there in your third-floor walk-up. New York. San Francisco. Muncie.

Forget the herd. Herd opportunities are passé. Teach yourself to fly solo. It's the future. It's good for the soul.

I have a very good friend who lost his job after Morrison Knudsen Corporation bought out the company he was running. My friend is an amateur pilot. A month after he was fired, he signed on with a volunteer food-relief program to fly a single-engine plane solo across the Atlantic and on to Somalia. By the time he landed in Africa, months later, he'd gotten as far away from home as he could possibly get. The very next step he took in any direction would only bring him closer to home again.

He stayed in Somalia for a year. Then he came back home. Bought back his old company. Expanded it. And he's still running it today. Why? Because he had the courage to break away from the herd, to break new ground.

How many history books are written about the crowd that stays behind? None. You've got to learn to be a pioneer, the one who makes a difference. You don't have to go to Africa. That's too easy. But you do have to learn to go it alone for a while. And that's the hard part. After that, it's time to write your own history.

· Standing at the Bus Stop with the Kids ·

Like my old grandma used to say, be careful what you wish for because you just might get it. Oh, to be home. To be able to spend more time with the family.

Well, now you've got your wish. You're a stay-at-home mom. A telecommuting dad. Call it what you want. It stinks. Standing in the rain with your kids waiting for the school bus. Listening to them shout to all their friends that their dad or mom has just been fired. Seeing all your neighbors rushing into the office. For what? *A steady paycheck*. Coffee with the boss. Meetings. Lunch. More meetings. Remember how you hated them? Remember how you couldn't wait to get home?

Don't give up. Not on yourself. And especially don't give up on the kids. They can be your best supporters and the best source of encouragement and, yes, good ideas. When my son was in middle school, he taught me how to make chicken stir-fry. It was the first time I was unemployed. It was the only thing I knew how to cook. The first thing I did around the house since I lost my job that actually made me feel good about myself. That made everyone else feel good. I have him to thank for that, not some career counselor or some outplacement guru.

Your children are your legacy. Unless you're planning on having someone erect a pyramid for you when you die, your children are what you'll be remembered for, not your career. Listen to them.

My brother-in-law is a very wise man. He was recently appointed chief justice of his state's supreme court. At his swearing-in ceremony, a story was told about a speech he had once given to the National Association of Attorneys General. In it, my brother-in-law spoke of his young daughter and something she'd once asked him that changed his perspective for good.

His daughter, who was five or six at the time, asked him who made the rule that you could only wish on the first star you see at night. Why not the second, or the third? It was a very good question. In a universe with an infinite number of stars, why limit yourself? Why be conventional? Why not break the rules and wish on all the stars?

Listen to your kids, he told the attorneys general that year. Forget the limits convention has put on you. Stretch yourself and multiply your opportunities. Sometimes kids know a better way.

· You'll End Up Living in a Box ·

There's no question about it. Money is the biggest source of hurt associated with a firing. It will cause you to lose sleep, make mistakes of judgment, affect your family. You have to tackle it head-on. Now. Before anything else. Here are a few helpful rules.

WHY DOES IT HURT?

RULE ONE. Don't worry. Be happy. I've tried it both ways. The don't-worry way is far superior to the alternative. Even if you're surrounded and outnumbered, it's far better to be cool and confident than stressed and sleepless. You'll be far more effective. And you'll be a lot more attractive to look at on that first interview without those dark circles under your eyes. Relax. You'll never end up in a box. You won't lose the house. Your kids will still get to college (as much as they'll probably prefer to miss the opportunity).

RULE TWO. Remember my son's happy/sad list? Make one of those for your financial assets. List everything. *Everything*. If your hand starts to shake and your eyes start to tear up, go outside. Take a walk around the block. Go by the playground and watch the kids play. When you feel better, go home and finish the list. Write down your hard assets and your soft ones. Cash and securities, as well as marketable skills. Anything that has financial value. It won't be so frightening when it's all right there in front of you.

RULE THREE. Consider handouts. Not the hat-in-hand subway station panhandling kind of handouts. Not the fifty bucks from your brother-in-law kind either. I'm talking legitimate, all-American, tax free handouts from Uncle Sam. Unemployment compensation. Poor man's venture capital. You've paid for it. Go get it. I promise you, more than one successful turnaround has been financed by government handouts. Why should yours be any different?

Go to the unemployment office. Right now. You won't be alone. Ask questions. Find out what's available to you. Once you check it out, you'll feel more comfortable about it.

RULE FOUR. Don't be satisfied with what you've got. Severance. Savings. Handouts. Go for more. Tell the bank you need a break from your mortgage payments for a couple of months. Credit cards? Car loans? When they call, tell them your sad story. You'll be amazed how far you can stretch things by just being open and honest. Remember how hard it was to get that mortgage? Well, guess what. It's even harder to lose it. Believe it or not, you're in the driver's seat now.

Another thing. Expect to end your unemployment with more money than you started with. I'm serious. Demand it, in fact. Don't give yourself a break. Do some consulting or temping while you look for a job. Help your kids build a lawn-care business. And remember, as my dad used to tell me, there's a million dollars for you out there somewhere. All you've got to do is find it.

· The Weather Sucks This Time of Year ·

It's true. There's no good time to lose your job. Wintertime is holiday time. The weather's bad. You can't go out of the house. Can't go to the beach. Summertime is when everyone else is at the beach, and you can't get anyone to return a phone call, or keep an appointment. Spring and fall? They're not bad. The kids are in school. The weather's decent. You can still get a good beach day now and then. Sound like a good time to plan on being fired?

Forget about it. The time of year and the weather are as unrelated to you and what you have to do with your life as talk radio. It's your life, and you have to get on with it no matter when it is. Weather. Climate. Geography. None of it matters. What matters is your attitude. And if the weather affects that, if you feel more empowered in the summer than in the winter, more energetic in the spring than in the fall, too bad. Life's not going to wait for you. There are no rain delays now, no snow cancellations, power outages. Unemployment knows no calendar. It's with you all the time. Every damned day.

What can you do if the weather doesn't cooperate? How can you jump-start your attitude? You can shut yourself up inside your house and not come out for a month. Or you can try some exhilarating moments. Exhilarating moments lift the spirit and inspire you.

Anything from a pleasant walk, a good workout, a movie, play, or book. Treat yourself to a hike in the woods. Climb a mountain.

I once heard the actor Dennis Hopper recommend getting laid to a workshop group that was discussing the staleness every actor confronts when he's been working too hard. Find something that works for you. Treat yourself to an emotional high. And don't let yourself give in to sucky weather.

· Sympathetic Injuries ·

I blew my knee out skiing a couple of years ago. Jackson Hole, Wyoming, Laramie Bowl, second run. When I got home I put so much weight on my good leg while limping around that it quickly became my bad leg. Watch out for this. Unless you're a hermit, your situation is going to affect a lot of other people, too. You owe it to them to turn unemployment into a benefit rather than a flaw.

Help out with the housework. Cook. Help coach the kids' soccer team. You've got the time. And I'm not talking sacrifice here. This is for you. This is selfish. Because the better you make your family feel, the better you'll feel yourself, and the quicker you'll avoid those unsightly circles under your eyes.

You've been banged around pretty good already. But

don't let your family get bruised too. Don't lean on your good leg so much for support that it becomes your bad leg. Just remember, nature encouraged this family thing so that we sad cats could occasionally be surrounded by happy cats when we needed them. But don't abuse the resource. Lean on your family, but not too hard.

Find something positive to tell your spouse when he or she comes home each day. Smile a lot at the kids. Every psychologist in the world will tell you that a simple smile elevates your self-esteem. Practice a little good humor around your family, and you'll see it reflected right back at you. Like a nuclear reaction, or that first morning yawn, one smile will generate another. And the smiles will feed on each other until everyone is feeling better. Be selfish. Smile.

· Summary of Things to Do ·

- Focus on positive actions; send a card to everyone you know, even the guy who fired you; ask for ideas, advice, and names of people to contact; follow up with a phone call; chances are, they'll want to help.

- Take some time to figure out who you are; make a road map of all the things you've done, successes and failures, victories and defeats; see where it leads you.

- Let go of the old and take control of the new; rearrange the furniture in your house, buy a new outfit, or try a course at night school; get a computer, fax, and e-mail; turn your kitchen into a virtual window on the world.

- Make a detailed financial plan; list everything: savings, severance, unemployment, and part-time income; attack expenses, the mortgage, kids' tuition, and car payments; talk to your creditors and ask them for a break.

- Listen to your kids; don't limit yourself; learn to wish on all the stars.

IV.

Sex and Expectations

January 20

What now? A résumé? Phone calls? But no one's going to want to talk to me. They all have things to do. Everyone has something to do except me. And even if they would talk, what am I going to say, what am I going to tell them? I was fired? Terminated? Laid off? Hell, I don't even know what I want to do with my life.

A very good friend of mine once explained to me that sometimes you get what you want only when you don't expect to. Things come to those who ask for very little. Like sex. You draw your partner a hot bath. Pour a glass of wine. Fix dinner. Help the kids with their homework. If your expectations are that this will lead to sex, forget it. This is what my friend taught me. If, on the other hand, you draw a hot bath, pour a cold glass of wine with no expectations whatsoever, this apparently is a *very big* turn-on.

The best method to get someone into bed also works well when you're trying to find a new job. Expect nothing. Be patient. People will find it much easier to find time for you, to offer you helpful ideas, if you don't push too hard. But don't forget that hot bath and the glass of wine.

· When You Get Knocked Down, Get Back Up ·

Remember Woody Hayes? The legendary Ohio State football coach? The winningest motivator since Moses? Woody Hayes was a tyrant. He took no guff from anyone. And one thing he absolutely insisted on from his players was that they never, ever give up. *When you get knocked down, you get back up.* Rule one. Before the cleats were laced and the helmets buckled.

Woody's team did a lot of winning in his day because Woody knew what was best for his team. What was best for us. You've been fired? Get back on your feet. Not tomorrow. Not the next day. Right now.

I've run a lot of start-up companies. And when I'm interviewing new hires, I always tell them there's a very big difference between small companies and big companies. In big companies, you can make mistakes because usually someone comes along, sooner or later, and fixes them. Otherwise the big company just slides through without anyone noticing.

In a small company, you can make mistakes also. So far things are similar. The big difference, however—and it's a *very big* difference—is that when you make a mistake in a small company, you must fix it. That's *you* and *must*. Because there's no one else to do it. And because every mistake, large or small, is potentially life threatening to a small company.

I've had to fire several people in my time. Not because of the mistakes they've made. But because of their failure to dig in and rectify their mistakes after they were made. Sometimes fixing your own mistakes takes more patience and stamina than anything else. But like Woody Hayes said, when you get knocked down, you get back up.

Right now you're in a very small company indeed. It's just you. No one else. The emperors and the bad guys have just beaten you up. Bad. But you must get yourself back on your feet. That's *you* and *must*. Rule one.

So, what do you do? How do you pick yourself up? How do you get the right perspective to enable yourself to fight back? The key is that first step. March straight into the bathroom and grin at yourself in the mirror. There's your answer, right in front of you. Remember that guy? That woman? Remember all the things he's

FIRED WITH ENTHUSIASM

been through? All the things she's accomplished in life? All the tough times? Births? Deaths? Hat thrown around the school yard?

Think about it. You don't have to make a list of all the things you've accomplished. Just take some time each morning to grin back at the person who's gotten you through so much in the past. Remember, you're not a quitter. You were fired. You didn't give up. The future promises to be successful because history knows you've succeeded before.

One step at a time. That's how you do it. Even Woody Hayes would tell you this. You don't win the game on a single play. It's step by step, play by play. The key is to undress the task. That's what we'll do in this chapter. Reduce the task to a series of simple steps and take them one at a time.

Remember, the first step is always the hardest. Like remodeling a house. Room by room. You start with the shabbiest room first, and save the one that needs the least work for last. As you proceed, you get better, more practiced. And the rooms require less and less work. Finally, the rooms that once seemed so shabby now gleam. And the once gleaming rooms seem shabby in comparison.

First step? Give yourself a big grin. And don't be tempted to accept that first job offer either. Take your time to do it right. Every step.

· Be Proud ·

I had a friend who moved to Boston from Ireland not long ago. He had a big job with a big company. Had a lot of people working for him, on both sides of the ocean. On his first weekend in the States, he and his wife went to a downtown pub. It was Saturday night. Very late. Yet the pub was jammed. They could hardly get in the door because there was a very popular local entertainer performing. A blues guitarist.

For an instant my friend and his wife almost turned away to leave. The crowd made it almost impossible to get inside the door. But they'd come 4,000 miles to a new city. What was a little more pushing and shoving? No sooner was my friend inside the door, however, than the guitarist on stage stopped dead in the middle of a song. He stared down at my friend and everyone turned. "There's the son of a bitch who fired me from my last job!" shouted the guitarist with a big Irish grin. "Launched my career in music, by God. Buy that man a Guinness!"

No grudges. No hurt. Just a proud man telling the world. Fired from his last job and glad as hell about it. It's a good example for all of us. Why let yourself be humiliated? Declare victory and move on. Who cares whose fault it was? Where you are matters to no one. It's where you're going that matters. History is only going to remember what you do next. Hell, that's all you'll ever remember yourself.

Be proud. How did that Irish musician do it? He found something he liked to do better than what he had been doing before and he figured out how to make a living at it. Sound simple? It's not. But it's a start. Make up your mind that there's something out there for you that will make you forget your old job. You're looking for something new because you *want* something new. Not because you were forced to. You fired them, not the other way around.

Give them hell, Harry! Remember that one? Harry S. Truman. United States president. Succeeded Roosevelt and helped win the Second World War. History regards Truman as one of the best presidents ever. An excellent leader. Pragmatic. Hands-on. But did you know that Truman was a failed haberdasher? That he didn't win his first elected position, a judgeship, until he was middle-aged? And he won that by only three hundred votes. An out-of-work haberdasher!

But Truman was a proud man. He refused to admit he was down. His pride was his greatest strength. It served him and his country well. It enabled him to turn his life around when he was fifty. Win a war and save a nation. From hats to president. Pride.

SEX AND EXPECTATIONS

· You Are What You Are ·

Bill Parcells. Two-time winning Super Bowl coach, with time out in between for open-heart surgery. The guy has more money than God. He can do whatever he wants with his life. But what does he choose to do? Coach football. Stare down the same stress monsters that drove him to his first heart attack. Why? When he first rejoined the coaching ranks of the NFL after a two-year "retirement," he said, You are what you are. And he's a football coach. He simply didn't want to be anything else.

How about you? Do you know what you are? Are you a fat kid or a skinny kid? Do you like big organizations, small organizations, or no organization at all? It's good to know these things about yourself. Maybe the reason you ended up in this predicament in the first place is that you weren't well suited to your previous situation. Round peg in a square hole.

Are you a competitor or a noncompetitor? When I was in college, I read an article written by the man who'd been one of the U.S. Olympic track and field coaches in 1964. In it he talked about competitors and noncompetitors. As an example of a real competitor, the author recalled Bobby Richardson, the great Yankee second baseman of the fifties and sixties.

The Yankees made it to the World Series a lot in

FIRED WITH ENTHUSIASM

those days. And year after year, Bobby Richardson would consistently bat better and have a higher batting average in the World Series than during the regular season. The tougher the situation, the more pressure, the better he performed. He was a real competitor.

As an example of a noncompetitor, the author talked about a boy he'd once coached in college. A pole vaulter who couldn't clear thirteen feet, a fairly respectable height in those days. The boy was an excellent athlete, had good style, and cleared lower heights by very comfortable margins. But he just couldn't break the thirteen-foot mark. And there was really no reason in the world why he couldn't.

One day, the vaulter's friends played a trick on him. They set the vault bar at thirteen feet but told the boy it was only twelve-ten. He cleared it easily. When he landed and learned what happened, however, the boy threw down his pole in disgust and stomped off the field. He never vaulted again. He was what the author called a noncompetitor. He worked far better in less stressful situations, situations where the limits were clearly defined.

Not all of us are competitors. For some of us, family is more important than work. And we aren't going to be happy in stressful environments that require every ounce of our commitment. Others are different. Like Bill Parcells, they are happy only when they are completely immersed in their work. Buried up to their ears.

It's important to know which one you are. Important to take the time to learn, so that you don't end up in a bad situation.

Take time, but don't take too much time. You'll learn a heck of a lot more about yourself once you make a start. Talk to people. Expose yourself to everything. You'll learn a lot more on the fly than you will on your own. That's human nature. People learn by doing. Just like children. Try things. Visit friends at other companies. Find out what makes their organizations tick, where the problems are, and the opportunities.

Maybe you'll discover you're more competitive than you thought. Maybe less. Maybe you're a big-company person. Maybe not. It may well be that you'll develop a real interest in working on your own once you've looked around. Maybe just the opposite. Maybe people are what will get your juices flowing and being alone is a torment. Be open-minded. Talk, ask, listen. But above all, listen to yourself. Use the time you have now to find out who you really are.

· Get-Even Lists ·

I had a friend who worked for British Telecom in London. He used to talk about a list of names he kept. On one side, he'd list all the people he liked, especially the ones he felt he owed a favor. The ones he'd go out of his way to do something nice for. On the other side, he'd list the people he owed in a different way. The jerks who'd done him wrong, at a time when he'd been forced to grin and bear it. He used to call this his get-even list. There was good getting even and bad.

Get-even lists can be counterproductive when you've just been fired with enthusiasm, however. Often you end up filling the wrong side of the page. You end up with many more names to skewer than to reward. Primitive aggression, remember?

Instead of a get-even list, what you really need is a go-get-'em list. A list of names of friends, business contacts, anyone who could possibly assist you in planning your next moves. The list doesn't have to be complete to make a start. But it's helpful to take the time to consider everyone you know. They will be your new allies, the people you'll lean on now. And it's a good idea to get their names on paper in order to see just how well off you are.

Who should you consider? How about customers, investors, bankers, headhunters, former coworkers, former competitors, classmates, neighbors, lawyers, relatives, parents of kids' friends, girl friends, boy friends, tennis partners, bar buddies?

Get the idea? The bigger the list, the better. If you have too many, you can always take names off the list later. And don't worry about what you're going to say. I can help you with that one too.

· Compose a Story and *Tell Everyone* ·

Remember the pride thing? You want to be proud, all right. Proud of what happened to you. Proud of the situation you're in. Everyone goes through it sooner or later. You'll be amazed how few people will think ill of you once you tell them. Just make up a story about it that you're comfortable with. Make it sound a little daring. And go.

"I finally decided to take the plunge and look for something new."

"I'm tired of making other people rich. I wanted to get out on my own."

"They offered a damned attractive package, so I jumped on it before anyone else did."

There. That wasn't so hard. Now pick up the phone and start talking. Take that list of names you made and start calling. Set yourself a daily goal. Three calls. Five calls. Ten. Start with something easy. Leave messages. Not just your name and number, but detailed messages.

Want to know a good trick? Call at 8:15 A.M. Most key people are in their offices by then. Frequently they'll answer their own phone at that time of day. Just call to talk. "Hi. I wanted you to know I just left IBM. I'm looking at a bunch of opportunities. I wondered if you'd care to have lunch? Spend a few minutes shooting the breeze. Just catching up. You know. I'd really value your opinion."

That's all it takes. You're on your way. Lunch tomorrow. Maybe a breakfast here and there. Slowly, you fill up your calendar. Remember sex and expectations. You don't ask for anything. You just want to talk. You don't tell them why you left your job. Just that you left. And you make pretty damned sure you tell whoever you call that you've always respected his or her opinion and you'd appreciate any help he or she could give you.

Tell them you value their suggestions. Got that? People love to hear it. I don't care who they are, how busy they are. You flatter them by telling them they're good, and they'll walk through fire to help you.

·Turn One into Many·

Okay. Now you're having lunch. Or breakfast. Maybe a morning jog with a lawyer friend. You tell your story. Add a couple of flourishes you picked up from one of your earlier phone conversations.

> "Remember Tony? I talked to him yesterday. He said my timing couldn't be better."

SEX AND EXPECTATIONS

You talk. You listen. Make damned sure you do five times more listening than talking. Encourage your friend to make suggestions. How? Silence. It's your greatest asset now. "What do you think I ought to do?" Ask the question and then shut up. Wait for as long as it takes. "Gee, I don't know," he'll say. Continue waiting. Like holding your breath under water. You can do it. If you master listening, the world will be your oyster. "You know, maybe I do know someone."

That's the way they will come. The first few ideas. No matter how painful it may seem at first, before long you'll be a master. Ever meet a master listener? Me neither. Most people don't have a clue how to listen. But once you're good at it, you'll be amazed how smart people will think you are.

Remember, it's not like college. They don't give tests. You can sit in a room full of quantum physicists all day, and if you just keep your mouth shut, they'll all assume you know as much as they do. Hell, by then maybe you will.

And don't forget the callback. To tell them how it went. How their suggestions panned out. Thank them. And use that silence trick again. Most people have their best ideas *after* they've met with you the first time. Something new pops into their minds the minute you leave. Or maybe the next day, the next week. When you call back to thank them for their help, no matter how it turned out, this is your reward. "Say, I just thought of someone else you ought to talk to." Bingo. Try to get two or three more names from everyone you meet. Milk them dry. Fill up two more pages. Don't stop until you've talked to everyone in town. Everyone in the state. Everyone on Earth!

· Indian Sprints ·

In many ways, a job is a liability. There's a lot more stuff you can do without a job than with one. You never fully realize it until you're in a situation like you are now. This is a great opportunity to get things done. Sprint to the front. Remember Indian sprints in high school soccer and track? Everyone jogs around the field single file. When the coach blows the whistle, the person at the rear of the line sprints to the front. Everyone gets his turn while the rest slowly jog.

Now's your turn to sprint to the front. No distractions. No one looking over your shoulder telling you what to do. You answer only to yourself. You have only yourself to please. Be honest. You were just plodding on your old job. Here's your chance to see what you can really do. Where you can really get to.

But don't start out too fast. Set yourself some easy goals at first. Goals you can beat without a killer effort. A couple of phone calls. A couple of letters. Get some victories under your belt before you go too fast. Remember, this is a story you're making up as you go along. And you just can't tell how it will turn out until you get into it. The start is what's important now.

Tell yourself you want to make ten calls a day. If you get them done by nine A.M., reward yourself. Take the rest of the day off. Treat yourself to a movie or a game of golf. Go to the beach or a ball game. Remember, what you do for yourself today will help determine how much you get out of yourself tomorrow.

Once you get started, how fast do you think you can you go? How far ahead can you get? Why not very fast and very far ahead?

I have a friend who left his job recently, leaving behind a crackerjack young salesman he'd hired just three months before. But without my friend's help and management, the young sales guy ran into trouble right away. His personality and style clashed with the others at the company, the same jerks who'd driven my friend to leave the company.

Before long, the young guy was fired. He was on the road in the Midwest. Cleveland. He went into a bar and ordered his favorite Irish beer. They had none. He went to another bar and another. No Guinness. Not anywhere in Cleveland. So the young sales guy sat down and decided. Cleveland. Guinness. In less than a year, he was Guinness's top salesman. Director of East Coast sales. Far ahead of the pack he'd left behind at his old job. Far faster than he himself ever expected.

· You're Only As Good As You Look ·

Take care of yourself. Exercise. Diet. Sleep. Getting into a self-maintenance routine early can be very beneficial. Not just for the body but for the soul. You might find yourself thinking better, feeling better, getting luckier. Remember the rich old guy who said he got where he was by being very lucky; and the harder he worked, the luckier he got? It's true. Hard work is what pays off. But pace and pitch selection will get you through more hard innings than anything else.

As petty as it sounds, statistics show that people who look good and feel good about themselves are generally more successful. I'm not talking hair transplants. I mean fatigue, dark circles. This new experience will be an emotional roller coaster for you. It will take energy, stamina, good posture, and eating from all four food groups.

The drill will be phone/write/phone/meet/write. First you call, leave a message, promise to send a résumé. Then you follow through with the résumé, wait a few days, and call to arrange a meeting. After the meeting, you write a thank-you letter. Then it's back on the phone to call the five new names you just got over lunch.

It's not easy. It can be grueling and demoralizing.

You have to be prepared. But you don't have to be perfect. You don't have to be an ooh-guy.

The ooh-guy is the candidate who shows up at the eleventh hour, when you've just about got a new job all locked up. He has a résumé that's so perfect for the job that everyone just goes "ooh" when they see it. What can you do about ooh-guys? Not a damned thing. Because worrying about ooh-guys is like worrying about a meteor bombardment. They're generally on a million-year cycle, strike randomly, and cause more damage than you could ever prepare for.

Take good care of yourself. But don't try to be perfect. Leave that to the ooh-guys.

· Summary of Things to Do ·

- Visit friends at other companies to learn new ways of doing things; incorporate what you learn into your own experience and discuss alternatives on interviews.

- Make up a story about yourself that makes you feel comfortable; script a sales pitch, then pick up the telephone and start calling; set yourself a daily goal of three, five, or ten calls; use e-mail and voice mail to increase your effectiveness.

- Make a list of everyone you know and contact them; if someone's hard to reach, try calling before 8:15 A.M.; ask everyone you talk to for two or three more contact names.

- Don't tell them you're looking for a job; ask for advice, ideas; then listen hard, coax them to tell you what they really think; learn to tolerate bad news; and afterward call back just to say thanks.

- Run harder than you think you can run; but avoid fatigue, dress right, and eat from all four food groups.

V.

How to Make It All Work

February 3

My first interview! God, what pressure. It's been years since I last had to do this. Like a first date. What do I do? What do I say? And my résumé? Is it right for the job or not?

So you've done all the dirty work. Burned the right incense. Landed that first interview. Now what? How do you play your cards to win? Remember, each hand is different. Each trick requires an appropriate finesse.

· The Résumé ·

In a world where no one has a clue, how do you convince someone that you do?

FIRED WITH ENTHUSIASM

Your résumé.

You've got all your past successes, victories, achievements in your database. You've created one giant text that tells your whole story, everything from the day you were born. Now you step inside your prospect's shoes and ask yourself the following key question: How can I get it all on one page?

Thus begins the process of customizing your résumé. Each new opportunity will weigh different factors in your background. Some will like your successes with key customers or projects. Others will like the fact that you flew solo in a single-engine plane across the Atlantic. Others may think it's great that you've run more than forty marathons. Some might even like your Wharton MBA. Every employer is different. Each one requires a customized version of your résumé to awaken his interest.

Once you figure out what the prospect wants to hear, just cut and paste until you have an answer for him. Keep it clear and concise. Use white space to draw attention to key facts. Consider using a functional format that highlights your accomplishments, more than just your places of employment.

Remember, the résumé gets you in the door. It's the single most important item in your quest. Until you land the job, it's probably even more important than you are.

· The Interview ·

The interview is like a distance race, so prepare and pace yourself. You've got to feel comfortable to make your prospect feel comfortable. If you feel stiff, he'll feel stiff. Remember back to the times you've interviewed job candidates yourself. What impressed you most about the good ones? Certainly, their knowledge and ability. But admit it, you already knew most of what you needed to know about knowledge and ability from the résumé. The rest you wouldn't believe anyway until you did a reference check.

No. What the interview showed you is what kind of person the candidate was. How he handled himself. How comfortable she was with you and with the issues of the new job.

Comfortable. The most successful candidates are the ones who make you, the interviewer, feel the most comfortable. When translated, this means they feel comfortable themselves.

How do you make yourself comfortable in an uncomfortable situation? A couple of stiff drinks? Maybe. There are lots of tricks. But one that you definitely don't want to try is racing frantically to make the appointment at the last minute, fighting traffic, arriving harried. It's much better to arrive early and treat yourself to a quiet cup of coffee, a relaxing lunch, a walk

FIRED WITH ENTHUSIASM

around town. Think about the things you want to say, the points you want to make about yourself. Write them down—a little checklist, what we used to call a "cheat sheet" in school.

When you're summarizing the points you want to make, don't forget the one about your goals and objectives. Sometimes we try so hard to fit ourselves to the specifications of a new job we forget we have to convince the interviewer that the specifications fit us. No one wants to hire someone he feels will be unhappy in a new job. So you have to make this point clearly and authoritatively. Just like any of your other qualifications, the fact that the job is perfectly in keeping with your own aspirations is very important.

When you finally arrive, when you walk into the interviewer's office, make it friendly. See if something nice to say pops into your head. "Lovely view." Or, "I can't help noticing that picture of your son in his soccer jersey. My kids play soccer too." Don't overdo it. Maybe the interviewer will start. "How was the traffic when you drove in?"

Remember, this is like a distance race. Let the leader set the pace. If he wants to talk about traffic, do it. "It wasn't bad at all. Twenty minutes on the freeway. No sweat." The success of any interview requires relaxing. Then you can more comfortably get your agenda across while moving at the interviewer's pace. If he wants you out of there in ten minutes, fine. Be relaxed.

Stay cool. If she decides you need to spend the day, meet scores of others, okay.

The same thing with conversation. You're a good listener now, remember? Listen for the rhythms of the conversation. Is the interviewer a big talker? I was in a three-hour interview once where the interviewer never asked me one question about myself. He talked and talked, about the company, himself. He took me on a tour, introduced me to every employee on two shifts. It was an ordeal. I found out later that he'd just received a résumé from an ooh-guy that morning. Remember the ooh-guy? His résumé is so perfect everyone just goes "ooh" when they see it. I think he felt so bad that he finally found his ooh-guy and no longer wanted me that he thought he'd better fill the conversation time himself. It was a very bad interview.

Normally, the interviewer will give you time to talk. He has to. Those are the rules. So don't think you have to force it. Wait your turn; use your cheat sheet. And if you forget something, don't worry. Follow up later with a letter. Thank him for his time. Tell her how much you really want the job, how well it suits your skills and goals. And then add the missing items. That's being thorough—a very good quality.

Now, the preparation. Each job is different. Each requires special preparation. I've discussed several key job categories below. Read them all. I think you'll find a little bit of useful advice in each.

· Sales ·

Sales is all about relationships. To position yourself properly for any new sales opportunity you have to convince your new boss that you know the right customers for his product or service—that if he hires you, you can deliver.

Sound heady? A guarantee? Well, it's not so farfetched. Not if you take your time to do the necessary homework. Before your interview or first meeting, ask for as much literature on the prospect's products and services as you can get your hands on. Read it in the waiting room if necessary. Talk with friends about the company. Find out what the new company's mission is and how it's perceived in its market. Get a feel for what its management team is trying to accomplish and who the right customers are.

When you know these things, when you know the goals and objectives and customer targets of your prospect, you're halfway there. Now get that list you made earlier of your own assets and resources. If you haven't already listed the customers you've been successful with in the past, do it now. Try to match customers and personal assets with the objectives of your prospects. Are there any good fits? Any stretches? Put yourself in your new prospect's shoes and rate them. Be honest.

Most new salespeople don't have a clue how to sell their company's products or whom to call on. I guarantee you, the person who interviewed ahead of you for the sales job you're after told the interviewer the first thing he'll do when he's hired is familiarize himself with his new company's product line. Hell, you're way ahead of him. You've already done that. You've read about it, talked about it to friends and former customers. You're armed for grizzlies.

The next thing he'll say is he'll get right to work with his new company's lead lists. That's not what I like to hear when I'm interviewing a new salesperson. You, on the other hand, impress me as a much stronger candidate. You already understand the product line and can start the job with leads of your own. You've even prioritized them. And, if you're smart, you may have even contacted some potential customers in advance of your interview, just to see what they think. The worst that can happen is that people will tell you the company's product stinks, in which case you can enlist some suggestions for improvement. Be a hero either way.

And if you happen to get very, very lucky and pre-sell one of your old customer friends on the company's products, you are in interview heaven. Then you tell the interviewer that if he hires you, you can just about guarantee him new customers. No one can refuse that. It's like passing up lunch with Cindy Crawford's cousin.

FIRED WITH ENTHUSIASM

Let's say you're not very, very lucky. Let's say your research turns up no one that can use the company's products right away. Nothing you've sold before is similar. The company's products are too unique for your past relationships to be valuable. That's no big deal. Why? Because relationships are relationships. People who can sell rye bread can sell computers. That's a secret no one knows but you. So you have to be convincing when you let people in on it—particularly interviewers.

How? Convince yourself first. Think about who the most likely targets are for your new company's products and services. The answer is probably in the company annual report. Think about how you would approach these prospects and find similarities with the way you approached your former customers.

Most of every ball player's home runs are hit on the same pitches over the same part of the plate. The only thing that differs from home run to home run is the ball. We all know what a sales home run is. And what I'm telling you is they're all hit the same way.

Work your way into the account by making friends, establishing relationships. Identify the customer's problems, what needs fixing. Sit down with your staff to figure out a way to solve these problems. Make an effective pitch. And be there, be there, be there with the customer. All the time. If you can't be there in person, be there on the phone, e-mail, letter. Make him think he's your highest priority. Hell, make him think he's your *only* priority.

The only thing that differs from sales home run to sales home run is the customer. Even the ballpark doesn't matter. If you've hit them before, you can hit them again. The secret of a good interview is to develop a way to show them you know how to hit. Examples are good. "If you gave me this job, I'd focus on the big commercial banks. I'd handle it the same way I handled Ford, GM, and Chrysler on my last job. I'd pick up the telephone and call people I know at . . ." You know how to do it.

In summary, study your prospect's products and services. Familiarize yourself with its mission and objectives. Identify potential customers and try to find parallels with other successes you've had. If you can hit a home run right away with someone you already know, someone you think may have an immediate need, call him up before the interview and discuss it. It's awfully nice to start a new job with your first commission check already earned.

· Marketing ·

Oops. Are you starting over from a bad marketing experience? When the dust settled on a really bad day, were all the fingers pointed squarely at you? Join the club.

Ever notice how the marketing luminary is always the first one to get canned when the fan gets hit? There's a corollary to this. Ever notice how few companies hit it big with the first product they set out to market?

Marketing success means changing your mind very fast without anyone knowing. So you've made some mistakes. If that's what's bothering you heading into your next interview, forget it. Most companies, departments, and new product lines run into problems. Things simply change too fast. And the speed at which they change has nothing to do with marketing. It has to do with CEOs and customers, most of whom have never spoken to each other.

What does this tell you? Be flexible. But how many organizations are truly flexible? Were they particularly flexible at your last company? There is no such thing as flexibility. There are only degrees of inflexibility.

So what do you do? In an inflexible world where customers change their minds like the wind direction, how do you position yourself? How do you market yourself for the next good opportunity that comes along? Listen. That's the answer. Listen to successful companies in your business and learn what kind of messages work for them.

Let's say you land an opportunity with a company in a new area of the industry, an area that you have little familiarity with. Let's say you have an interview with the CEO or a senior VP for an interesting marketing position. What do you do? How do you prepare?

HOW TO MAKE IT ALL WORK

Try a little research. Identify the biggest competitors to your new prospect in his markets. If it's not easy for you to do that, ask the prospect himself. Before your interview, when you call to say you want to stop by to pick up a bunch of his product literature, ask him who he perceives his competitors to be. Then pick up the telephone and give them a call. Check their Web sites. Find out what their message is. What's their strategy and focus?

From the literature packet you receive from your prospect, see if you can figure out how he currently attempts to position himself relative to the competition. Are there any holes in his logic? Any strong points? Next, try to talk to a couple of potential customers, people you think might need your prospect's products or services. Find out how they perceive the messages the various competitors pitch.

Now you're ready. You're not only prepared to talk about yourself, but to talk and listen about your interviewer's needs. Don't forget to listen, even during your interview.

But how do you listen when it's you that's being questioned? Be patient. Wait your turn to ask questions. When the time comes, use the research you've just done to script a couple of questions that will not only show that you know your prospect's business, but that you know how to think out good solid marketing solutions. Listen to the answers to your questions and frame additional questions around these. Remember, an interview is just another opportunity for valuable market research. What you learn in this interview will help you on your next. And the more you learn, the more effective you'll be when you finally land that job.

When I was CEO and interviewed new marketing people, I wanted to find candidates who understood my customers. I wanted to find individuals who could develop a strategy and articulate a message that would make a customer want to buy from me, rather than from my competitors. And I wanted individuals who could spot trends and alert me to them before anyone else spotted them.

When you are interviewed, you have to convince the interviewer that you have these skills and abilities. You have to build his confidence in you. And in order to do that, you have to have confidence in yourself.

Anyone can come in and say he'll conduct more expensive research and spend more money on advertising. But if you come in with an understanding of his markets and ask insightful questions about his customers and competitors, if you listen to his answers and give him back solid ideas, then you'll be in a much stronger position to differentiate yourself from the one-stop wonders who think marketing is all about wearing bow ties and jacking up the advertising budget.

· Finance ·

Now here's an interesting dilemma. You're the corporate tail gunner, the one no one else wants to see or hear. You operate out of sight, behind the scenes. But you'd damned well better be there, on the job and ever vigilant, or the plane is going down in flames for sure.

Yours is the driest of all professions, stoker of the corporate boiler. You don't exist unless things go really, really wrong. You never get credit for success, but always take the blame for failure. On top of all of that, you're always first in line to deliver the bad news, to CEOs, directors, and department heads. You're the messenger that every emperor wants to behead. And now, after getting blamed for every layoff and firing that's ever occurred, you find yourself in the unpleasant position of having to sell yourself. So how do you it?

The answer is you have to convince a new employer that you can do the impossible, guarantee there will be no surprises. If you don't, someone else will, and he'll be the one getting the job.

The impossible? No way. But think again. Just how impossible is it? No surprises. Ever vigilant, like radar. Did you ever think about radar? Little blips fired off into infinity. Very simple physics. And if there's something out there, the little blip bounces back and bingo! Everyone finds out what it is in time to do something about it.

Here are the two qualities you need to sell yourself: the radar quality and the tail-gunner quality. Nothing sneaks up on you, and nothing gets by you. All problems are identified while there's still time to shoot them down. And they *are* shot down. In flames. No survivors. Make the point convincingly, and you'll have the job. I promise you.

When I interviewed CFO candidates, the quality that most impressed me was the ability to shrug off the biggest demons I faced. "Run out of cash? No way. I'll build a plan, monitor performance weekly, put tight controls on purchases, travel, advertising, inventory, everything. You fly the plane; I'll watch for missiles."

Sounds great. But what about finding new investors? "No sweat. I've worked with some of the best. Hell, I play golf with some of the folks at XYZ Capital. I'll put together a plan that will get them in here next week. And let's get things squared away with the banks. I'll set up meetings next week. I'll handle them myself. You can concentrate on other stuff. In my last company, we were hemorrhaging cash, but I quickly hammered out a new line of credit and a workout plan."

To be successful in finance, you must be perceived as an instant good night's sleep. Most CEOs and top managers are clueless about their problems, where they are, where the money is going. Show them that you know. You've seen it all before. Nothing can surprise you. Name names. Tell war stories. But above all, show how you build a plan and develop controls, how you send out radar blips and get them back again. The simple truth is, yours is an easy job. But no one else at the company dares to do it.

· Research and Development ·

The glory days are over. Ten years ago, R&D whizzes were considered godlike. Millions were thrown at every bit fiddler, physicist, and DNA sleuth with a business plan. Not anymore. People have gotten smart. Translation: They never could figure out how to sell what you designed for them in the past, so they've done the only logical thing. They've dumbed down the technology.

Now you find yourself competing with programmers who create code by selecting objects like Chinese menu items. One from column A, two from column B. The only agencies funding important research are the motion picture studios. And even defense department electronics have been preempted by computer games. What do you do? Where do you take your talents?

If you want to save your soul, go to Tibet, study to be a Buddhist monk. If you want to save your career, look for stuff that's like the stuff you did before. Not the same products, but problems that require the same elegant solutions. Every R&D vice president wants to be convinced that what he needs done you can do in your sleep. A five-finger exercise. As easy as rolling out of bed. So don't disappoint him.

Remember a good interview is all about telling the prospect what he most wants to hear. The hard part is figuring out what that is. Well, listen, because I'm going to tell you. Every R&D manager wants to be a hero. He wants to get the project done, on time, under budget. And he wants the product to work the first time out of the box.

But let's be honest. Walking into an interview, flashing your résumé and saying "no problem" to every question the prospect asks is probably not going to get you the jobs it used to. Now you've got to be a little more specific. "This project is very similar to one I just finished for Bell Labs, Eli Lilly, IBM"—fill in the blank. "I realize my last project required launching a satellite with a slingshot and you're looking to cure the common cold, but there's significant relevance."

Now it's up to you. "Each project requires a database and, boy, do I know databases." Or "Each project requires the development of sophisticated computer modeling. I just completed developing the modeling algorithm of the century . . ." You get the idea. Find the common ground between what you've done before and what they want you to do now and convince the prospect you have all the experience to do it again with no missteps.

Another thing: Try to be normal. Coat and tie. Nice dress. Shoes. There are still a lot of R&D types who show up to interviews looking like they just rolled out of a fraternity party. Frankly, it's scary. In a world where people are looking for any excuse to flunk you, you certainly don't want to give them any easy ones.

Also, it helps to portray the image of the careful carpenter. Measure twice, cut once. As R&D VP or CEO, I'll not only want to know that you consider my new project routine, but that you will treat it with the care and vigilance of the kids' physician, the corner-crossing guard. No swashbuckling.

· Information Management ·

Computers. Yuck! Anyone who spends a career in information management certainly deserves the Johnson & Johnson award. You know, for most Band-Aids used. After spending every waking hour tweaking and bandaging your company's computers and networks, you find yourself looking for something new. The only problem is, have you managed to stay current with everything else that's happening in an industry that

FIRED WITH ENTHUSIASM

moves at the speed of an Indy car race? Are you able to jump in and manage someone else's data? If not, then do as my college roommate always suggested to me. Study some more. Chances are, you'll need to.

If you've spent your career managing Oracle databases, chances are your first three interviews are going to be with companies using Sybase. If you've always worked in UNIX, you'd better be ready for Windows NT. Mainframes? PCs? Out of luck. Laptops and handhelds are the rage. And networks? Forget about it. WAN. LAN. Satellite. Wireless. Ethernet. Token Ring. Novell. Hub and spoke. Switched. Routed. You can't possibly know it all. Or can you?

The answer is, you probably can, and should. It's never too late to pick up the leading magazines in your area of expertise. The ones you were too busy to read on your last job. Browse the Internet. Never before was it as easy to learn about new information technology as it is now. Every vendor of hardware, software, and networking glue has a Web site. Every one of them offers seminars—*free* seminars.

Call and tell the vendor company you're working as a consultant and have clients interested in his technology. It's easy to get seminar invitations. And it's a very productive use of your time, too. Not only will you learn the latest and greatest in technology, but chances are, you'll also pick up some good job leads. Make friends on both sides of the podium. The person giving the

HOW TO MAKE IT ALL WORK

seminar and those in attendance are both good sources of job ideas or consulting opportunities.

The vendor wants to be your friend because you may land a job somewhere where you can convince management to buy the vendor's products. He'll be impressed that you'll want to know about all the latest improvements and bug fixes. And the attendees will love you because you'll listen to their problems, offer free advice, and tell some good jokes over lunch.

Now you know it all. So what do you do to hit a home run in the interview? Every CEO and CIO wants to be convinced he has no problems. All that computer downtime? "It shouldn't be happening. No, sir." Flaky software? Network outages? "I'll say it again. It shouldn't happen."

And tell him *why* it won't happen with you on the team. Like the plumbing at home, everybody wants the information network running smooth. No leaks. No blockages. Make sure you focus on how smoothly things went back at your old shop. Relate little successes. Don't talk about monumental systems crashes where you saved the day by employing a lot of Band-Aids and long hours. Cut directly to the solution and explain all the systems crashes that were avoided because of it.

Employ your new knowledge of the hardware and software he uses. Remember how attentive you were during the free vendor seminars you attended? Chances are the interviewer didn't have time to attend himself. Chances are he knows nothing about those new improvements and bug fixes you took such careful notes on. Chances are he'll be impressed as hell that you can tell him things he didn't know himself about his own system. Nice job. Good hunting.

· Project Manager ·

You're captain of your ship. Not quite fleet commander. But in some ways you're much more important. You leave port each day and take the frigate into combat. You're the one who knows what's going on. Right or wrong, win or lose, you make it all go. You have to be the expert, the leader. You have to know how to stoke the boilers, fire the cannons, man the wheelhouse.

What do you do to prepare for that first interview? Make sure you know the prospect's stuff—the product, technology, or service—inside and out. You cannot expect to be successful competing for a project management position in a field that's new to you. There are simply too many other good candidates for you to get a foot in the door. Like the R&D candidate, you have to tailor your résumé to fit the interview. Find similarities between the work you've done before and the products, technologies, and services you'll be working on now. If you're successful, chances are you'll know more than the interviewer himself. That's good, if you present yourself properly. Successful candidates I've met have been able to talk to me on a broad range of topics within my field. Hardware, software. The physics and logic behind the hardware and software. Industry standards and regulatory bodies. Market trends and futures.

Glean from what you already know, and research the stuff you don't. Find a friend in a similar industry and have lunch. Ask if you can come by and visit at work. Pick his brain for everything he'll tell you about the industry. Be a sponge. Soak up every detail. Talk to engineers and developers. Find out what's current, what's hot. Then be prepared to tell the interviewer more than he knows himself about his own company's area of focus. Know all the pieces and how they fit together. Show how they relate to the pieces you've worked with before, the pieces you have experience with. Then show him you can thread the loopholes.

Loopholes. Anyone can manage schedules where everything runs smoothly. The trick is to convince the interviewer that you can make things run smoothly when they're not.

How do you do this? Again, experience helps. War stories. Many candidates come into interviews with long lists of past projects delivered on time, on budget. That's good. On time and on budget is good. But it doesn't really tell me a whole lot about you and how you work.

What you need to tell me is how you managed to deliver on time and on budget. Don't just tell me about the problems you solved. Tell me about the ones you anticipated, the corrective actions you organized *before* things went south.

To get the job, you need to prove to me you're organized, articulate, resourceful, and—here's the hard part—likable. Because unless you work alone in outer space, virtually all project problems are people problems.

Product development running late? People problem. Critical piece of equipment late or broken down? People problem. Customer changing his mind about key features? Union going out on strike? To solve them all you've sometimes got to be a cross between Vince Lombardi and Mother Teresa. I've seen some candidates I couldn't leave with my plants for the weekend. They had personalities that would wilt lettuce.

· CEO ·

So, you would be emperor? Good luck. The field of opportunities definitely narrows at the top. The last company I worked with had three employees who were former CEOs. Each had more than ten years experience as a CEO. But guess what. Not everybody could be chief. Two had to be Indians. Guess how that made everyone feel.

To be a successful CEO candidate, you really ought to start the company yourself, have no partners, and take in no investors. Then you have a chance. A small one. Knowing someone, such as the owner, or even marrying the owner's son or daughter doesn't do it anymore. Nine out of ten new companies fail. That means that for every CEO who's employed, there are at least nine more experienced CEOs looking for work, circling like sharks waiting for someone else to fall overboard. And since new CEO positions are as rare as hen's teeth, that means that there are at least ten thousand experienced candidates for each new opening. Who wants it?

The CEO is the poor slob who answers for everything. Customer complaints. Shareholder complaints. Directors, employees, vendors . . . simple logic says that there's no way for the CEO to have a happy day. You can't please all the people all the time. The minute you move from managing some of the people to managing all the people, your blood pressure redlines. And it doesn't come back down until you're fired or your company fails. Sound inviting?

There was a very sad, very sobering story in the financial newspapers last year about a middle-aged man who spent many years working for the same large company. He was a very successful, conscientious executive who worked his way up the corporate ladder until he was finally appointed to the top position. But luck was against him. His corporation ran a nationwide chain of restaurants that saw its customer base erode within days of a lunatic shooting spree at one of its restaurants. Within three months of his appointment, the new CEO was so distraught over the sudden downturn in his fortunes that he took his own life.

Everyone wants the top position. Probably everyone reading this book has at some time or other dreamed about the top spot, the front office, the emperor's throne. I can't help you. I've been CEO twice myself. I've felt my blood pressure redline and come back down too many times to think life at the top is really that healthy.

It's a very lonely job that you absolutely cannot do by yourself. In many ways, the CEO does nothing. He's the ultimate delegator, or ought to be. Because of that, because he has to rely on others for every success, he has no real control of his situation. It's like being on a train—or worse—a roller coaster with no track.

· The Follow-up ·

So you've had your interview. Met the troops. Sniffed the bait. Now comes the hardest part. You wait. What is it about waiting that drives a human nuts? Look around you. Pets can wait. Dogs. Cats. They spend their

HOW TO MAKE IT ALL WORK

lives waiting for the next meal, the next car to chase, the next mouse to torment. Ever seen a cow running around the barn clamoring to get milked?

Why us? It's the grim downside to having a brain. A brain generates thoughts. And when you're unemployed, nine out of ten thoughts are worries. To paraphrase Descartes, you wait; therefore, you worry.

I'm afraid I can't offer any alternatives. Frequently, if you do anything but wait, you'll torpedo otherwise good opportunities. Don't appear too anxious. We are descended from hunters. Millions of years of them. And a hunter likes to hunt. He doesn't like to be hunted. Remember dating? The thrill of the chase? It's the same thing for interviewers. They don't want you bugging them until they've made their decision. Give them time. Often an interviewer will give you a far rosier picture of the decision cycle than is really the case.

Don't be a pill. Write one letter after your interview. Call a week or so later. Then try to put the opportunity out of your mind. It doesn't hurt to call infrequently. But not more than once every couple of weeks. People get tied up on other things. Priorities change. And an ill-timed phone call or e-mail can send a harried executive into a funk about you that no amount of skill, knowledge, and personality can untangle.

· Summary of Things to Do ·

- Custom fit your résumé to every opportunity; check your list of victories and assets and pick the ones that fit each interview; be brief, get the most from the fewest words.

- Read the company's annual report and its product literature; visit its Web site; figure out how the company is structured, what its goals and expectations are, and how it positions itself relative to its competitors; sell yourself to fit the company's needs.

- Attend free seminars, both in your field and in other fields; learn about new products and trends; make contacts on both sides of the microphone and talk about yourself to everyone.

- Arrive early for interviews and take a short walk, listen to some music, and relax; follow the interviewer's pace, don't rush and don't be rushed; make a list of questions and points about yourself you want to make and refer to it during your interview.

- Wear a suit and tie or nice dress and polished shoes.

- Show them that you've seen it all before; use examples from your old job to fit the new one; borrow from things you've learned on other interviews, from reading product literature, from attending seminars or from visiting other companies.

- Don't be overanxious; be cautious with your followup; remember, people are busy, schedules get changed, and nothing happens as fast as you want it to.

VI.

What to Look for in Them

February 17

An offer! A real job. But should I take it or not? I'm so hungry for work I'd jump at anything. But I can't let myself jump without being sure. The people, the company. What do I really know about them?

As important as it is to prove to an interviewer that you're a good match for his company and needs, it's even more important to prove to yourself that the new company is a good match for you. The last thing you want is to take a situation that will make you unhappy—or worse.

You don't want to be forced to compromise your values. You don't want to be forced back onto the street looking for work just because your new company unexpectedly ran out of cash. And you don't want to be so embarrassed to represent your new company and their products that it affects your work.

When you look at a new employer, consider the intangibles. What are the company's values, personalities, style, even its logo? Are they right for you? Will it be a good match, or agony? The right amount of investigation now can save you a lot of unpleasantness later.

· Values ·

I once ran a company that provided services to state and municipal governments. Contracts were generally written for several hundred thousand dollars and required a sealed-bidding process lasting several months to qualify.

During my first few months on the job, one of our top sales people came to me with a dilemma. A manager for a key municipality had just disclosed to our salesman the amounts of our competitors' bids submitted for a critical project. The municipal manager wanted to be sure our company won the project and that the price was affordable to him.

He should have saved himself the trouble. Our bid, which hadn't been submitted yet, was lower than any of the others. And the opportunity was in a sales territory where we would have worked extra hard to perform well because we were so eager to establish a beachhead.

WHAT TO LOOK FOR IN THEM

But with very little reflection, I chose to submit no bid. Through no fault of ours, the integrity of the bidding process had been compromised. And to knowingly participate in a fraudulent process was just not right.

I was wonderfully relieved when others at our company supported me. There wasn't a single person at our company who disagreed with my decision, including the salesman.

Values. I guess I found out then that I had some. And it was comforting to know that my fellow executives and staff did, too. From that experience I learned that common values are an important criterion in choosing bosses and fellow workers.

There is a much quoted piece of advice that says if you want to be a world-class athlete, the first step is to choose your parents very carefully. The same can be true of seeking happiness and success in your career. Choose the people you work with very carefully.

Remember John Scully? He ran Apple Computer for many years then left to join Spectrum Technologies, a wireless communications company that some felt was on the brink of a breakthrough technology. Within twelve months, however, the Spectrum bubble burst. The company's principals were indicted for fraud, and Scully escaped with a very tarnished reputation and a very bitter lesson learned.

Reputation. After your children, it's the most important thing you have. Don't mess with it, even in the desperation of a job search. How do you avoid mistakes like John Scully made? As my father used to say, some people are plain unlucky, and the dumb ones are the unluckiest of all. You can't do anything about luck. But you sure as hell can be smart when it comes to checking out a new employer.

Everyone in the wireless industry was suspicious of Spectrum. And a thorough investigation would have found the truth. The company was barely profitable on very modest revenue and a very skimpy service offering. Yet it had a market valuation of hundreds of millions. Unless the company was sitting on the breakthrough technology of the century, it appeared to be nothing more than a shell game. Even the experts thought so.

Make it an important part of your homework to be certain the people you intend to work with have the same values as you. Check with others in the industry. Check with competitors, customers. Carefully sift what you hear and make a thoughtful value judgment of your own.

· Personalities ·

In my last company, I made the mistake of partnering with a man who had no personality. He was honest, hardworking, had a heart of gold, and was very, very

=== WHAT TO LOOK FOR IN THEM ===

smart. But the poor man was dry as old toast, and it got to be very difficult sticking it out with him.

Work ought to be fun. Life ought to be full of color, not gray shades. The weekly paycheck isn't all we're after. We want to be noticed, to feel good about ourselves. A laugh, a friendly slap on the shoulder is what we're after, not silence, frowns, closed doors.

There's a well-known story among management researchers concerning a test that was conducted at a very large General Electric plant thirty or forty years ago. In it, researchers experimented with the brightness of lights on a large assembly line. During a period of several weeks, researchers continually increased the brightness of the lights, and measured productivity as they did.

The brighter the lights grew, the more productive the workers got until the researchers attempted to test the test by turning the lights down again. During another several-week period, therefore, the lights were slowly dimmed. Guess what. Productivity continued to rise. In fact, it rose and rose until the brightness was less than it had been when they started.

The moral? Pay attention. Productivity rose, not because of the lights, but because management for once was paying attention to the poor slobs on the assembly line. Everyone felt involved. Work was fun. Life was grand.

If the people you intend to work with show no interest in you and aren't themselves interesting, if they don't like to laugh and can't make you laugh, forget about them. Life's too short to get started with them. Believe me. The main reason I'm writing this book today is because I tried and failed to stick it out in an organization with no personality.

I once told my partner my GE light-test story, by the way. It seemed to strike a nerve. For a minute, he actually seemed intrigued. He wrinkled up his nose and thought about it. Then he turned to me and asked, "Were they using incandescents or fluorescents?"

I rest my case.

· Style ·

Style isn't something you find on the pages of *Vogue* magazine. It's the way you do the things you do, the methods you employ to achieve success.

Style is determined by a variety of factors. We learn style from our parents, teachers, corporate mentors. We try things, see which ones work for us, which we are comfortable with. And slowly, over time, we establish a style that is uniquely our own.

Individuals have style, and teams have style. When joining a new team, it's critical to know that your styles match. If you're a three-point shooter, you will be miserable playing on a team that insists on posting the ball.

WHAT TO LOOK FOR IN THEM

If you're a quarterback with a golden arm, it will be agony to play on a run-oriented offense.

Style. It has to fit your new team and your new market. I once worked with a company that hired a sales vice president from a similar segment of the same industry we were in. The new sales VP had achieved considerable success selling data communications products to *Fortune 500* customers. When he joined our organization, he was asked to sell our data communications product to the same customers he'd already demonstrated so much success with. Easy, right? Wrong.

The previous product our new sales VP sold was a $5,000 piece of hardware. Our product was a $250,000 piece of software. Each product required a unique selling style. The old product required lots of salespeople making lots of sales calls. Our product required a few salespeople working with a small number of customers over a very long period of time. Peddling versus relationship selling. Completely different styles. The new sales VP was an all-star on one team and a chump on ours.

Make sure you're walking into a situation where your style won't clash with theirs. Sometimes, even the interviewer won't know. The CEO who hired our new sales VP came from a peddling background himself. He had very little concept of what it took to establish the relationships necessary to sell our product. And he compounded his ignorance by hiring people like him.

In chapter 4, I discussed the importance of knowing

who you are. Are you a fat kid or a skinny kid? Is your style geared more toward company A or company B? Take the time to be sure.

· Logos ·

Will you be embarrassed to represent your new company? Is the corporate headquarters the kind of place you'll look forward to coming to work in every day? Is the product one you'll be able to brag about? Believe it or not, these things can matter as much as salary and benefits.

In one of my early ventures, I teamed with a very bright, very eccentric physicist who insisted on naming our company after his favorite animal. He designed our logo himself, with a very prominent and very homely wolf's head. And for the first several months, I was too embarrassed by the logo to give any of my business cards to new prospects. Not a very promising way to conduct sales calls.

One day, I gave up. I hired a graphic designer who transformed our wolf's head into a truly compelling graphic. I was so excited, I had T-shirts printed up for everyone on the staff. And the company grew like wild in the years after that. Did the new logo help? I think it did.

A not-so-famous basketball coach once told me, *"You can't make chicken salad out of chicken shit."* If chicken salad is what you want, chicken salad is what you should look for. That means all the ingredients are important. Product, logo, corporate headquarters. Pride of ownership is what you want in your new job. If you don't have it, your performance and happiness will suffer. So don't settle for anything less.

· Runway ·

How much money does your new company have? Is it likely to go out of business or undergo painful layoffs right after it hires you? Just because it has a job opening and is interviewing, don't assume it really knows what it's doing.

One of the most painful experiences I ever went through involved ordering the layoff of an individual two months after one of our managers hired him. The manager who did the hiring left the company within weeks of hiring the individual. Shortly after that, we discovered significant cash-flow problems in the manager's own department, which required immediate cutbacks. The experience made me more skeptical of the hiring/firing process than I'd ever been.

Try to find out as much about the new prospect's financial stability as you can before you're hired. When it's your turn to ask hard questions of your interviewer, find out if his company is profitable. When was the last round of financing, and how much was raised? How many employees does the company have?

Although it's a very rough gauge of a company's prospects, most companies should be able to generate at least $100,000 of revenue for every employee. And don't accept projections. *"We expect to do $25 million in revenue next year."* Great. How about last year?

Ask the hard questions. But don't be unreasonable with the answers you'll accept. Many of the most exciting job opportunities you find may come from start-ups that employ twenty-five or thirty people, that generate less than $1 million in annual revenue, and that haven't been profitable since the day they were founded. In their case, their value is in their potential. Then your questions should focus on their staying power. Who are the investors? When is the next round of financing going to occur? How much money have you raised in the past? How many more new employees will you be hiring? And when do you expect to be profitable?

The potential, and the risk, of these small companies can be great. Find out how much runway they have left. If you weigh all the factors and decide that the potential outweighs the risk, don't forget to ask for additional compensation to allow you to participate in any gains the company's future growth may bring. Ask for stock options as part of your compensation package.

Stock options give you the opportunity in the future to buy stock in your new company at today's prices. If the growth potential is great, your options will be worth substantially more than you pay for them. Options typically "vest" over a three- to five-year period. That is, the longer you remain employed, the more options you will be granted. Stock options are a great way to take the sting out of jumping into a risky venture.

· Summary of Things to Do ·

- Don't be forced to compromise your values; next to your family, your reputation is the most important asset you have; look for the same qualities of honesty and integrity in a new boss that you demand in yourself.

- Find out what it takes to be successful at your new company and match your style and personality to the company's; look for personalities that will be stimulating, people who can inspire and lead, leaders who can tell chicken shit from chicken salad.

- Check the company's finances, history, and projections; find out how fast it's taking off and how much runway it has left.

VII.

Starting Up

March 11

Maybe a job isn't what I really want. Maybe I need to go it alone. Hell, I've always wanted to be my own boss. Start my own company. Buy a franchise. Build a consulting business. But how? Where do I start?

We've talked about interviewing and the preparation for interviews. But what if a job is not what you decide you want? What if what you really want is to travel the path less frequented, to start your own business? This is my favorite subject, what I've spent the past twenty years doing myself. Start-ups. Life in the fast lane. Or maybe it's the breakdown lane. But never the cruise-control lane.

FIRED WITH ENTHUSIASM

AT&T recently announced a layoff of four thousand employees. Not very big news these days, I'm afraid. What was big news, however, was that part of the severance package AT&T offered included $10,000 for each outgoing employee who was interested in starting his or her own business.

Now, $10,000 will not put any new venture on the gravy train. But the idea is unique. If one of the largest corporations in the world is ready to invest $40 million in the entrepreneurial endeavors of a bunch of people it just fired, maybe there's some merit in considering entrepreneurship for yourself.

So, how do you start? What do you do? What kind of business or service do you consider? Unless you have very deep pockets or a breakthrough product idea, you really have one choice. Consulting. Offering to do for others, on a part-time basis, what you've been doing for your previous employer on a full-time basis. It doesn't matter what you do. Sales. Marketing. Development. Finance. Regardless of what some emperor thought, you have talents that others can use.

The math works in an interesting way on consulting too. Generally, you can charge more per hour than you were making on your old job. You work more efficiently because you no longer have the interruptions of corporate life. And because you get more done in fewer hours, your client ends up paying you less than he would pay for a full-time employee of his own.

Now you can spread your time over more than one company. By working more efficiently and productively, you may be able to handle two, three, or more clients simultaneously. And by having the additional experience that your work with multiple clients will bring, you can increase your value to each of them.

Sounds great. So how do you find these clients? One method that I found works well is to team up with others. People like yourself looking to launch themselves as consultants. Even better, find someone who already is a consultant. It's better to have the experience behind you than to team with a bunch of rookies.

But why will anyone want to team with you? For the same reason you want to team with them. To expand the field of opportunities.

· We Few, We Happy Few, We Band of Brothers ·

This quote from Shakespeare's *Henry V* has always been a favorite of mine. It is engraved on a very important rowing trophy my college team successfully competed for long ago. And it has stuck in my mind because the value of teamwork has always been important to me.

Starting up is first and foremost about teamwork.

Forming teams with new clients, teams with new partners. In the consulting business, perhaps more than others, teams are vital because of the way each consulting professional works. Head down, immersed in a project like hand-to-hand combat. The closer he is to completing a project, the harder it is to pull himself away, to start lining up the next project, the next piece of work.

That's why it pays to partner, to team. Everyone keeps his eye out for everyone else. If I'm busy in Company X, working on software development, I may hear of an interesting marketing project that one of my teammates could use. Or, perhaps one of my partners might hear of an opportunity I could move to when my current project ends. Perhaps you'll discover that it's worth keeping one person as a full-time salesperson, paid out of the project fees he finds for his partners.

The point is, we all need someone to lean on. And if you can't afford to start a company from scratch, how about a return to communal living? Everyone contributes his time and energy for free. Everyone keeps what he earns for himself, but looks out for his partners in the process. Forget about salaries and finder's fees. The venture capital of the new millennium will be freely contributed time to ventures such as this.

· The Virtual Company ·

The next step, after the communal venture, is the virtual company. You've got your consulting work and a handful of teammates. You've been hanging out in the market for a while, making some money, feeling good about yourself. Suddenly you find yourself so well positioned in the industry that you're able to spot some interesting new trends and ideas. You sit down with your teammates to discuss these new trends and ideas, and suddenly a product idea jumps out at you. What the market needs is a better, inexpensive kayak.

This is a true story, by the way. A good friend of mine, a man who worked with me on an earlier start-up, began a project such as this with his partners. They created a virtual corporation for building and selling kayaks. They are now a world leader.

The way they started was simple and inexpensive. They had no seed capital, so they used the next best thing, the freely contributed services of professionals like themselves. More teammates. One person contributed design services. One contributed production facilities. And everyone, in return, became shareholders in the virtual corporation.

The story of the kayak manufacturers is useful, not just as an exposé on virtual corporations, but as an interesting case study on being fired with enthusiasm. The two principals of the company came together about five years ago after some painful career restructuring. One had been laid off from a long career in manufacturing. And the other was feeling trapped beneath the corporate-opportunity ceiling.

One of the partners got the idea for a durable but inexpensive kayak while reading an outdoor magazine. He took the idea to a professional kayak racer who also happened to be a design engineer. The engineer fashioned a unique, patentable design while the partners found a manufacturer of plastic containers that desperately needed work to fill his factories.

A deal was cut whereby the original two partners teamed with the designer and the manufacturer to build a couple of prototypes. The designer contributed his design and engineering experience. The manufacturer contributed his factory, workers, and materials. And the original two partners contributed the legwork necessary to find the first distribution channels. Today Walden Paddlers, Inc., still employs only a handful of workers while selling thousands of kayaks through magazines, catalogs, and outdoor stores across the country.

The virtual corporation worked for them and is an ideal vehicle for bootstrapping one of the good ideas that may come out of your consulting consortium. But what if your team comes up with a great idea for a product or service? What if taking advantage of this great idea requires more than the efforts of a small team? Instead of a virtual corporation, what if you want to build a real company?

· Investors ·

Investors dress sharp. I put that in there for my mother who said I should always try to find something nice to say about everyone. Try extra hard, she used to say, if you need their money. And to start a real company, you'll need their money.

Investors. Damned if you do, and damned if you don't. They're tough to find and tough to keep. I've had good experiences with investors and bad. The bad experience has largely come when investors have tried to do more than invest. There is no question that the assistance of market-savvy investors is critical to any new company. The only problem is I've never met a market-savvy investor. That's why I offer some caution. To paraphrase ZZ Top, beware the sharp-dressed man. Or woman.

Thus warned, let's proceed. Your new product idea has rocketed out of the consulting consortium, soared past the virtual corporation, and now the only way to keep it growing is with the infusion of some real capi-

FIRED WITH ENTHUSIASM

tal. Now you have to be a writer. Now you need a business plan. You need to describe in writing your product, your technology, your service so that even an idiot can understand it. You have to dissect your market and your competitors, plan your growth, your people needs, your capital needs. You have to describe your advertising plan, your sales plan, your financial plan. And you have to project everything at least three years out.

And remember, a business plan is not a porn magazine. You can't put the sizzle in the middle. What's so hot about your new idea? Why is it going to make everyone rich? All this has to go up front, because that's all that may ever get read. All the work you put in the guts of the plan is worthless if you don't grip the reader early. And gripping these readers is very hard to do indeed.

Investors see hundreds of business plans. They usually read only one in ten. Most of the plans they read are discarded. About one in three hundred becomes an investment. And one in ten investments fail. Still interested? Why not? I rolled the dice three times myself. Each of the companies is still in business, in one form or another. But now I'm writing a book about being fired, so you decide.

Angels. These are wealthy individuals who invest on a whim. Successful businessmen and women, doctors, dentists, lawyers. Friends. Relatives. Angels typically invest in small multiples of $10,000. They will occasionally ask to sit on your board of directors and will hound you miserably at cocktail parties because they'll never really understand your business. But they'll want to.

Angels are a good first step if you are looking for $20,000 to $100,000 of seed capital to finish your research or your design or to buy a critical piece of equipment.

Venture capitalists operate at the next tier. Although some venture firms will participate in seed investments, they typically invest in multiples of hundreds of thousands and millions of dollars. For many millions, you will need many venture capitalists, which isn't so bad because venture capitalists like company on an investment. Like kids on the end of a pier all waiting for one intrepid soul to take the first plunge, they'll all pile on an investment once the first one jumps.

Venture capitalists will insist on taking board seats. They'll ignore you at cocktail parties. They'll never really understand your business either. But they won't care a twit that they don't. Venture capitalists are in the game for the "long haul," until the company gets sold, goes public, or fails. And if you decide to work with venture capitalists, keep a copy of this book nearby.

How do you find them? It's best to have a reference. Everyone knows someone who's a venture capitalist.

Bankers. Lawyers. College roommates. You'll need someone, because the chances of getting to first base with a VC go from slim to none if you don't know someone. As for me, I didn't know anyone, so I had to be resourceful. I partnered during my consulting stints with people who did. It pays to choose your happy band of brothers carefully.

Banks. Bankers are the sharpest dressed of all, if you get my drift. Bankers will typically invest only in your real orders. They'll loan you only the money you need for equipment and inventory. Only for hard assets that they can sell if you go bust. Bankers don't sit on your board. They don't hound you. The only time you ever hear from them is when your loan is called. No warning! Just before the doors are padlocked. And that's why your finance tail gunner is worth her salary.

· Finding New Employees ·

Now the tables are turned. You're the emperor. You're the one running the new company. You're the one creating new jobs. What kind of people do you look for? What qualifications do you seek?

There are a couple of important things to keep in mind. New hires, particularly your first new hires, are

STARTING UP

the people you'll rely on most. Like it or not, these are the folks who'll make you or break you. Business is a team sport, after all. And this is especially true of startups. The more your company succeeds, the more it grows, the more you lose control. But you *want* to lose control. You want to delegate it to key people. You want to stop being the player and start being the coach.

Ever notice how many great players make good coaches? Very few. That's because it's very hard for them to give up control of the game, hard to extend themselves and their skills through their players.

Starting up requires a considerable amount of perseverance and ego. By the time you've built up your company to the point of hiring your first employees, you've already enjoyed a certain amount of success. You've already put out your share of fires. And the temptation is to believe you can solve any problems. Like the great player, you think you can do it all yourself. As a result, you let your guard down hiring new people. A very big mistake.

Don't look for people with narrow focus and limited expertise. Hire people who are generalists, who can tackle a variety of problems and seize opportunities others might miss. Don't recruit people who are used to large organizations and their infrastructures. Find people who are resourceful, adaptable, and self-reliant.

Resourceful. Look for people who can think on their feet. People with what my college roommate used to call "soil intelligence." Common sense. I like to think I have resourcefulness. And I definitely look for it in the people I hire.

Last year, I made a sales call on a very large account. One of the top ten corporations in the world. My partner and I went in together, made our presentation, and then sat through a long discussion of why our software product wasn't appropriate for the new customer. The customer had existing software that was slower but satisfactory. Ours was expensive and lacked some of the features the customer was determined to have in a new product. To make matters worse, this customer had no time or test equipment to test a new software product. That was April. A flat no.

By the end of the year, we had a quarter-million-dollar order from the customer and nearly one thousand of their sites installed.

How did we do it? Resourcefulness. We wrote a software test plan and built a piece of test equipment ourselves. We hunkered down, wrote the necessary enhancements to our software, and returned to the customer's site to install the test equipment and the software to run the test for the customer ourselves.

Resourceful. Where one person hears "no," another hears something entirely different.

Adaptable. How many successful companies actually end up providing the same product or service they started out making? I asked this question earlier.

STARTING UP

Adaptability is what got you where you are, and it's an important quality to look for in the people you hire.

In 1914, the German army invaded France and launched what became the Great War, the most costly stalemate in history. But the Great War was very nearly a one-month rout instead. The French army, trained to fight the Germans from highly fortified positions in the east of France, was outflanked and routed in the first month. The Germans rushed around the French forts, drove the French army into panicked retreat, and were within miles of Paris when suddenly the French wheeled around, dug themselves in, and reinvented themselves as trench warriors. The ghost of St. Genevieve? Perhaps. But still one of the most stunning adaptations in history.

New companies more than any other need to be adaptable. Business plans often turn out to be wrong. Money tends to run out sooner than expected. New projects fail to materialize. A host of bad things can and will happen. What do you do? Dig in and fight. What do your employees do? They damned well better be there in the trenches, too, to help you come up with new ideas—fast. That's what they're there for. Tell them that up front. During their interview, ask them what they'd do if the business plan turned out to be wrong. If the money ran out. Make them sweat. See how adaptable they are.

Self-reliant. Remember the corporate coat of arms at

your last company? Cross your arms and point one index finger north, the other south. Then recite after me. "He did it."

Unh-unh. Not anymore. "He did it" becomes "I can fix it." Right away. You need employees who can keep things running, on their own, without supervision or the support of a big company infrastructure. I once made the mistake of hiring a salesman who wouldn't go on a sales call without bringing along an engineer to answer the technical questions. Six months with the company and he still didn't feel "comfortable" going out on his own. Guess what I did. I fired the salesman and moved the engineer to sales. Much more efficient. Much more effective.

Success or failure, you'll be the one who'll be remembered for the results. But I can tell you from experience, your success or failure will be driven more by the hiring decisions you make today than anything else you do tomorrow.

· Stone Walls ·

So what path do you take? Consulting? Partnerships? Virtual corporations? Venture-backed companies? This morning while I was out running, I had to duck into the woods for a pit stop. Before I came back out to the road, I happened to look around at the picturesque stone walls that threaded the woods and fields around me. Where did they come from? Who put them there and why? We all know they were put there by farmers during the first couple of centuries of settling New England. But why? Aesthetics? To mark boundaries?

I remembered an article I'd once read that said the reason for stone walls was much less dramatic than people thought. The walls were put there because farmers needed some place to put stones that were taken from their rocky fields. And since it was too much trouble to haul rocks any further than the edge of the field they came out of, the stone wall became a kind of dump, the nearest convenient spot to pitch annoying rocks before plowing and planting the field.

Three hundred years later we cherish our stone walls. We use them as natural boundaries for house lots and roads. To that the early settlers might say, "Great, but all we really wanted was a place to dump rocks."

Maybe that's all you need to get yourself started. Not some breakthrough idea, some one-of-a-kind product or service. Maybe you just need something to do, a convenient place to dump rocks. Who knows? History may look back on what you did as having true merit, like the stone walls of colonial days. But as the old farmers themselves might say, why should it matter?

· Buying a Business ·

Buying an existing business can lessen the agony and uncertainty of going it alone. Every major city has reputable business brokers who can help you consider what's available. Business brokers operate like real estate agents and are generally compensated by the seller. A business broker can help you choose a business from lists of what's available, or he can team with you by searching for the specific business that you want.

Some cash is required to purchase a new business. But generally a major portion of the purchase price can be "earned" from future revenues. Like paying off a mortgage, you can pay off the original owner over time from earnings realized from the business itself. The initial valuation should reflect an amount that the business itself can sustain. That is, most businesses can be expected to pay for themselves.

Often, however, this payback cuts into the salary you can pull out of the business for yourself. So you should consider purchasing a business while you have alternative means of income available to you. These can be severance, unemployment, savings, and so on. In considering the purchase of an existing business, therefore, be prepared to work for yourself for free until the business is paid off. When it is, you not only can

STARTING UP

begin to take a salary for yourself, but you also will have accumulated a valuable piece of equity for yourself and your family.

The value of purchasing an existing business is the business's name, its facilities and equipment, and its customer base. You are paying for and should receive a significant amount of capacity and goodwill for your money. That is, you should be able to get right to work, day one, with an existing customer base, earning real revenue. Any business that has an unknown name and no backlog of business is no better than a start-up and is not worth any price.

A good alternative to starting a business from scratch or buying an existing business is to purchase a franchise. As with other alternatives, purchasing a franchise requires an initial cash outlay. This will be for inventory, sales materials, and for the cost of purchasing or leasing a space for the business.

In addition to the initial cash outlay, there will also be an annual fee paid to the franchiser himself. Like the earn-out in purchasing an existing business, the franchise fee is an annual amount taken from the earnings of the business. In the case of a franchise, however, the fee buys more than just the business and its goodwill. It purchases an ongoing commitment from the franchiser to advertise and market its name.

In purchasing a franchise, you become part of a national or regional enterprise and secure instant benefits from its name recognition. Your success will be driven largely by the overall success of the franchise. Opening a franchise, therefore, is more like working for a large company than either the start-up or existing-business alternatives.

· My Experience ·

The first company I helped found followed the path I outlined above. So did the last one—from consulting to virtual corporation to venture backed. It's still too early for a verdict on the newer company. So far, it's done quite well. We started out as a consulting group about five years ago. We came up with a product idea, a software product, about three years ago. And we bootstrapped the development of the product and our first Wall Street installation ourselves.

About two years ago, we wrote a business plan and brought in several million dollars of venture-capital investment. The venture capitalists took several board seats and brought in their own management team. We landed some key accounts, hired about thirty people, and seemed poised for real growth.

Earlier this year, I was forced out of the company by my partner and the new management team. They told me my heart was no longer in it, and they were right. The venture capital brought with it a management style and layers of structure I found stifling. That's the problem with the raptures of self-employment. I enjoy being my own boss. I don't like emperors trying to tell me how to buy horses.

As for my first company, it had an even more twisted saga. We developed a very interesting bit of data communications technology back in the eighties. Then our company ran out of capital in 1987. But before we did, we pioneered a product that is still being sold. Thousands of our products have been purchased, and our technology helped to launch an industry. Versions of the high-speed computer architecture that we developed in the eighties can now be found inside a variety of products that form the foundation of a robust $6 billion market.

I'm very enthusiastic about my start-up experiences. But they aren't for everyone. On the one hand, I've managed through the years to keep up a steady source of income. I've been my own boss and have done some really creative things. On the other hand, I now claim to be *the* expert on being fired with enthusiasm. I leave it to you to decide for yourself the right career path to pursue, big organization or small, mature company or start-up. Right now, the world is your crap table. Just make sure you have the wind and the stamina to stay the game.

· Summary of Things to Do ·

- When starting out, multiply your effectiveness by forming teams; partner with others like yourself to form consulting groups; keep what you earn, but share leads, contacts, and experience.

- When it's time to build a company, consider a virtual corporation; bootstrap your efforts with the free contributions of others; give everyone a share in ownership, but pay no salaries until your product or service generates real revenue.

- When raising money, put lots of sizzle in the front of your business plan: an exciting product, a unique service, or a breakthrough idea; get the reader's attention right away before he tosses your plan on his growing stack of rejects.

- When you start to hire, look for people who are resourceful, independent, and bring good relationships with them; find someone who can hit a home run first time up at bat, someone who can come right in with a new idea, a key customer, or a major investor in his pocket.

STARTING UP

- Beware of success; too much growth can bankrupt, too many customers can stress, too much structure can restrict.

- Consider buying an existing business or a franchise; look for a known name, good references, and a strong order backlog; find something that will pay for itself in three to five years.

VIII.
Marathons and Long Walks

April 3

I'm tired already. I've pushed myself hard. And they tell me to be prepared for this to take months. No stone can be left unturned. Nothing's unimportant. Everything is priority one. But where will I get the energy?

I know I promised to write what I know about firings and enthusiasm. But right now I want to talk about marathons and long walks.

Marathons. I've run a lot of them. More than forty. And I think the experience relates to finding jobs. In the early miles, we're all a little giddy, a little crazy, a little scared. In the middle miles, we settle in. We experience lows and highs and more lows. We try not to think about how far we've come or how far we have to go. We keep our minds riveted in the present. Toward the end, we often hit the wall. No more energy, just sheer determination. Stubbornness.

Long walks cleanse and elevate the spirit. So do cooking, home repair, and playing with the kids. Remember, it's better to soar than to mope.

· Giddy and Scared ·

The early miles. This is the easy part. Five miles. Ten miles. Everything looks bright and rosy. Lots of energy and enthusiasm. Just like the early days and weeks of a job search. You get out and reconnect with people you haven't seen in years. Ideas pop up. New leads develop. The air is alive with possibilities. And above all, you're free of the pack at last. Right?

Wrong. The early stages of a marathon are nowhere near as rosy as this. You feel aches and pains everywhere. Weak and stiff. And above all, you think you've made a very big mistake just being out there.

The same is true for the early days and weeks of your job search. Life couldn't be worse. You feel lost and depressed. In the morning your body still wakes up on time for work. At night you feel you owe the world an explanation for all the things you didn't accomplish. You feel like the last surviving commando, lost and alone behind enemy lines.

MARATHONS AND LONG WALKS

This is where you need to set some goals. Right away. Make some lists. Names. Phone numbers. Get your financial analysis done. Set some easy goals and declare some early victories. This activity will help you cut yourself loose from the old regimen. Help you launch a new one. It's a lot like traveling to Europe. The first day, you feel like crap. But if you hang on, make yourself adjust to the time change and the new currency, things will be fine.

· Highs and Lows ·

The middle miles. If things seemed bad early, they only get worse now. Aching muscles stiffen. Fatigue starts slowing your progress. You feel like you've been at it too bloody long and still have too bloody far to go. This is when you really want to quit. Right?

Wrong again. By the time you hit the middle stages, you've settled into a routine. Some miles are better than others. Some days deliver some really exciting prospects. Some days deliver crushing disappointment. The real difficulty of the middle miles is keeping emotions on an even keel.

Don't let yourself get too high with the highs, or too low with the lows. Keep fueling your enthusiasm with a good steady-state effort. Ten phone calls a day. One or two meetings. If one meeting goes really well, don't stop to celebrate, don't let it keep you from making your other calls. If a job opportunity that seemed really promising fails to materialize, don't let yourself go into a funk. Whether you overtake the race leaders or get lapped by them, don't let anyone else on the course affect your running.

· Heartbreak Hill ·

People think I'm crazy. I know they do. Twenty-six miles. Why expend the effort? Because the marathon provides something that's just not available in everyday life. The chance to achieve a difficult but well-defined objective.

The Boston Marathon is commonly considered one of the hardest runs anywhere, even though, for the most part, it's not a difficult course. It's predominantly downhill and run with prevailing west winds at your back. Moderate temperatures. And a race-day crowd of more than two million spectators to cheer you on. Hell, it's like a big party.

But Boston has one immense obstacle that confronts the runner at the very worst time of the race. Heartbreak Hill. From mile eighteen to mile twenty. It's a backbreaker. If you hit Heartbreak feeling strong, it can still melt your energy like a Popsicle in the sun. Hit Heartbreak feeling spent, you can end up in a medical

MARATHONS AND LONG WALKS

tent. But make it over, and you're home free. The last six miles, tough as they are, roll downhill to the finish.

The dark beauty of a Heartbreak Hill lies in the challenge of planning for, confronting, and beating it. Every year, it's right there where you expect it. It never moves. Never gets bigger or smaller. And that's why I run. Because nothing else in life is so well defined.

That's why marathons are easier than job searches. In a job search, you're never done. No matter how much planning and confronting you do, how much heartbreak you survive, you're always still going either up or down. But keep at it. Keep setting those goals. There are few spectators in the race you're running. You've got to be your own coach, your own cheerleader.

One Father's Day, my sons gave me a card that I've always cherished. On the cover it said "Let's Hear It for Dad." On the inside was a battery and a little speaker with a white-noise generator. Open the card, the battery drove the speaker. The white-noise generator made it sound like a room full of friends clapping and cheering for me. I still keep it in my desk. Sometimes I open it just to remind myself that I'm still winning as long as I'm running, even though the top of the hill seems miles away.

· Hitting the Wall ·

Sooner or later, the marathoner runs out of gas, hits the wall. He's made it more than twenty miles. Climbed Heartbreak. Fought the highs and lows. But somewhere before the finish, he simply depletes all his energy. His body runs out of glycogen to fuel the muscles. It's like nearing the end of a long, fatiguing drive. Hundreds of miles on the highway. Then running out of gas and having to push the car the last five miles.

I've hit the wall many times. In marathons and in life. Sometimes near the end of a very long effort, everything hits rock bottom. It's the hardest time of all. No matter how far you've come, how close you are to the end, hitting the wall can knock you down so low you want to quit.

I can clearly remember a very long ordeal on a previous job search. I'd been at it nearly eight months. I'd had many meetings, many interviews, and had even tried some consulting. Nothing looked promising. It was winter, and a very good friend of mine was nearing the end of a long illness. As he failed, so did my spirits. The day he died, I hit the wall. I felt like all my energy went in the grave with my friend. I wanted to give up.

That day was the lowest. And the next day was pretty bleak, but not so low as the first. The day after that and the next and the next were better still. I was hurt and staggering, but I could feel myself recovering. I began to think about life. I began to think about *my* life. Began to see that what I'd been doing, looking for a conventional job, was wrong for me. I was an entrepreneur. I'd had some ups and downs, but that's what I was. And it took the death of a friend and hitting the wall to make me realize it.

Within five months, I had another start-up. I was a founder again. Real customers and revenue. And even though there would be more ups and downs, I was happy just to be on the roller coaster again. I'd found what I needed to do. Not to work for someone else. But to be my own boss. And the thing I learned is that sometimes when you hit rock bottom, you're really where you want to be.

· Listening ·

Ever hear a runner interviewed after winning a big marathon? Invariably someone asks him what he thinks about for twenty-six miles. How does he keep himself from going nuts? Ever hear what they say? They listen. Listen to their bodies.

What a bizarre thought! When was the last time you really listened? Were you even listening when the emperor fired you? Probably not. Probably had so many voices shouting in your ears that you couldn't hear a thing. What will my wife say? My husband? How will I pay the mortgage? The kids' tuition? How will I face the neighbors? A hundred voices.

But in front of two million screaming spectators, the marathoner says he listens to himself. How is that possible? I'll show you. Take your thumb, press it against the wall as hard as you can. Now try to ignore your thumb. You can't. It hurts. As long as you press it hard, you can't help but be aware of it. The same is true of the marathoner's body. It takes no effort of will to listen when you're pressed. It comes with the territory.

Unemployment can create the most stressful situations in life. Panic. Rejection. Isolation. Take advantage of it. Learn to listen like the marathoner. Learn who you are. It will help you listen to others. It will help you solve the riddles of the job search. Help you find opportunity where it's hiding.

The early bird may catch the worm, but only if he's a damned good listener. I've worked with a lot of early birds who couldn't catch a worm if you hung it on their noses. To paraphrase the shrink from an old Mel Brooks routine, listen to your worm. It will tell you how to catch it.

· Long Walks ·

Every once in a while, you have to stop and walk. That's my secret to longevity. Long walks, to me, are the equivalent of meditation. Mental lubrication. If my mind is cluttered, or I'm feeling stressed, I set out for twenty minutes or a half hour. Winter or summer. And I try to think about nothing. I just let my thoughts drift.

It's an ironclad, guaranteed way to recharge your batteries, to generate ideas, to get a new perspective. When you work on your own, job hunting, writing, starting a new company, a good long walk is like calling a meeting of your key staff. Collecting input, fueling creativity.

Why does it work? If you think about it, our species has been sedentary for only a very short portion of our existence. Remember those 2.5-million-year-old tools? When you consider that man was agrarian, working his fields from dawn until dusk right up to the time of the Industrial Revolution, our time spent as desk-bound office potatoes is only about 1/10,000 of all man's time on Earth.

That is, if the entire history of man's existence was a single twenty-four-hour day, our time spent as desk-bound office slugs would occur only in the last eight seconds before midnight. That means we have a 2.5-million-year history of taking long walks. From the prehistoric savanna to Central Park, man has been on the go.

Movement settles the nerves. Calms the mind. Lets all those thoughts and ideas we know are buried somewhere in our cluttered minds drift to the surface. Besides, why argue with history? When you're feeling a little mental constipation, lace up those shoes and let the thoughts flow.

· Standing on Your Hands ·

Remember high school shop class? Remember that guy who taught us woodworking, metal bending? Turns out he was a genius. He knew something about history even the dry old farts teaching Latin and Greek had forgotten. What differentiates our species from all others? Our minds and our hands. Hands. There's something even the Latin and Greek teachers may have forgotten. Work one without working the other, you tip the apple cart.

Working with your hands is a great way to dissipate stress. Just as good as taking long walks. Ever notice how doing something as simple as washing the dishes or raking the lawn can relax you? I remember learning this lesson during a particularly stressful period of unemployment. At the end of a frustrating day, I was feeling very down. No one was home. I was climbing

MARATHONS AND LONG WALKS

the walls, ready to jump off a bridge, except there were none where I lived at the time.

In my yard was a pile of old lumber left over from the demolition of a shed. Hundreds of rusted nails stuck out of the boards. And I was concerned for the safety of the neighborhood kids who seem drawn to old wood piles like three-piece suits to Wall Street. My wood pile was just waiting for a kid and a lawsuit, but I'd been avoiding doing anything about it for weeks.

Finally, feeling at rock bottom, I grabbed my claw hammer and attacked the debris, nail by nail. At first, it seemed like the dumbest thing in the world. After all, I had my future to worry about. What the heck was I doing standing in the yard pulling nails from old wood? In about ten minutes, however, I started to get into it. A nice, calming, repetitive motion. Pound, hook, pull. I began to relax. It had rained earlier in the day, but the clouds suddenly parted and the sun came out. I felt relaxed, at peace.

After about a half hour of nail pulling, I was able to get back to the house and work again. I accomplished more that afternoon after my respite with my hammer than I ever could have done in the mental state I'd been in before. Like giving myself a mental massage. My mind was stimulated. Because I'd worked with my hands!

· Seek and Mingle ·

You're on your own. Day after day. No one to look at. No one to talk to but answering machines and bill collectors. You've tried walking, running, mowing the lawn. You still feel down. Stale. You need something more. Either a sudden, unexpected job offer to make life right, or just to get out and mingle.

If you feel like this and that job offer continues to elude you, then run away from home for a while. Put down the phone. Shut off the computer. Go somewhere where you can see people again. Girl watch. Guy watch. It's good for your mental well-being. It helps you remember that you're not the last person on the planet. That you belong to the species—a species that is, for the most part, happy, resourceful, and attractive.

Try something else. Call someone just to talk. Not a job thing. Just a date. For coffee and a chat. Tell him or her the good stuff and the bad. See how much better you feel. Ask him what's new, and practice that new trick you learned. Listening. See how much better you can make someone else feel. And pat yourself on the back again. Heck, you're getting good at this. A little unemployment has made you a better citizen. Someone is sure to want to hire you now.

· Fun Things to Do While Unemployed ·

We are judged by the things we do, as much as by who we are. Suddenly, unemployment has given us the opportunity to be judged in a new way. What do we do with the time we have? Besides writing, calling, and listening, what other things can we do to nurture ourselves and our souls?

GO BACK TO SCHOOL. Unemployment provides a wonderful opportunity to sharpen skills or to develop new ones. During a recent term of unemployment, I took a screenwriting course at Harvard. It was a terrific opportunity. It opened pockets of creativity inside me I never knew I had. Will I ever sell a screenplay? Who cares? What I learned in that course transcended the old make-a-buck logic. I learned to see things more clearly. I learned to express myself more succinctly. I learned to dream. None of these things will go on my résumé. But they will help me feel good about myself, and that's very important.

REMODEL A HOUSE. I have a carpenters license. I've had it for more than ten years. I got it shortly after selling my first company. I was burned out, tired of people, politics, and office work. I needed something that would refresh my spirit to the point where I could even begin to think about looking for work again. My wife and I purchased a run-down old house, and I took myself to school. I tore out every wall, every plumbing fixture, every electrical outlet. I rebuilt, replastered, rewired, and replumbed the entire house in six months. My back problems and excess weight vanished. I learned enough to pass the state licensing exam for carpentry. And I refreshed my spirit enough to head back into the business world for another stint.

VOLUNTEER. Help a friend out with a business. Do hospital work a couple of afternoons a week. I tried coaching my kids' soccer team once and fell in love with it. I quickly realized that the physics of team sports is very much like the physics of business. Think about the problem of trying to convince a bunch of nine-year-old athletes to work together to win a soccer game in the pouring rain. No salaries. No bonuses or stock options. Just for the fun of it. Learn how to do that, and no people problem at the office will ever seem so hard again.

THROW A PARTY. Want a good lesson in logistics? Try organizing a surprise birthday party for your spouse, in your own house, for one hundred people. Sound like good training for later life? It is. Everyone wants to be invited, but no one wants to help. Just like back at the office. I was out of work, so I couldn't afford to be extravagant. I couldn't afford to rent a hall, so instead of taking my wife to the surprise, I had to bring the surprise to her. It was my finest hour. I rented a yellow school bus for the evening, had all my friends meet the bus at a supermarket parking lot, just like high school. They decorated the bus, got some birthday music. And at the appointed time, I coaxed my wife into the driveway in time to see our friends arrive like eight-year-old kids in a bus full of balloons and banners and champagne. It was very cool.

WRITE A BOOK. It's no big secret. That's what I'm doing right now. Unemployed and writing about it. Writing is a great way to unlock your inner self, to learn who you are. And it has really helped to put the process and the predicament of unemployment in focus. Try writing a journal, a log of your thoughts, your ideas. It doesn't matter if you can't think of anything to say. Picking up a pen and paper, sitting down at the word processor is the best way to make ideas come.

Back to school, carpentry, volunteering, throwing parties, writing. It doesn't matter what you do, what you try. The point is, doing is better than moping. Maybe you'll uncover some valuable new resource inside yourself. Maybe you won't. But just because the emperor kicked you out, he has no damned right to sentence you to idleness. Get started. Have some fun. You deserve it.

· Summary of Things to Do ·

- Don't get too high with the highs or too low with the lows.

- Don't let anyone else on the course affect your race.

- Be your own best cheerleader.

- Don't give up when you hit the wall.

IX.
The Jerks You Leave Behind

April 12

I never realized how good I had it before. Boy, I miss the old gang at work. I'd give anything to have this all over with, just to be back where I was. But who am I kidding? They probably don't miss me a bit. Probably everything's running a hell of a lot better back there without me. I guess the thing I'd like most is to find another group just like the one I left. The devil you know is sometimes better than the devil you don't.

When things are rough, it's sometimes good to look back and remember how much better off you really are. Better off without the jerks, the dead men walking at your old place. We all know who they are.

· The Emperor ·

We've already talked about emperors. They're the ones in charge. Who think they are, anyway. That's why they're so insecure. Because they're not always as much in charge as they'd like to be. They usually sit in their offices all day, playing video golf or something on the computer. And every once in a while, they run out their door in a panic demanding to know what's going on.

Why is that? Why is it emperors don't have a clue? It's because they're too high and mighty. Too far removed from what's really going on. Remember when you started your career? Entry-level coding? Sales? Production? Remember how things worked then? Someone gave you something to do, and you did it. Just like that. And when you were done, no one knew more about the thing you just did than you.

Next you moved up to management, and you gave projects to other entry-level people. When a VP or director stopped to ask what was going on with the project, you had to ask the person who was working on it. And so on. As you progressed higher in the food chain, you knew less and less about what was really going on. Then you became the big boss. The emperor. And you didn't have a clue. Sound familiar?

Emperors have another problem. Ever hear the body-parts joke? In the joke, the body parts argue over which of them should be in charge. The brain says it should be him because he's got all the intelligence. He runs everything. The lungs say, nonsense. Without us, the body would die in a few minutes. The heart says, a few minutes? Without me, the rest of you would be dead in seconds.

Then from down below, the asshole can be heard chuckling. Want to know how long it would take to die without me? Want to know what *that* would feel like? Yuck. And the discussion quickly ends. That's why, no matter how many ways you look at it, how many times you argue, the asshole always ends up in charge. That's why so many emperors are such . . .

· The Master of Disaster ·

Remember this one? The guy who lights all the fires just so he can be a hero putting them out? The woman who fails to order a key piece of equipment just so she can save the day by getting something in at the last minute?

Hustlers. That's what the emperor calls them. Wheel spinners is more like it though. They run around like chickens with their heads cut off. They take ten hours to do what anyone else could do in three. No feet up on the desk with them. Just a cloud of dust and hours of unnecessary work for everyone else.

The real beauty of masters of disaster is how they

tend to keep the emperor busy and out of everyone else's hair. After all, every disaster requires the emperor's involvement. Right? Even if it didn't, the master would involve the emperor anyway, just so he could show off. To paraphrase the Zen masters, is a disaster really a disaster if the big boss doesn't know about it?

With a master of disaster on the staff, you definitely don't want to get your own work done on time, without a glitch. You'll look like you're dogging it. Like you don't care. Maybe that's what got you fired in the first place. Emperors and masters.

· The Go-Getter ·

Ever hear the story of the go-getter? In the morning he takes his wife to work. At night he leaves to go-get-her. There's usually one of these guys in every office. You probably had one back at the old place.

The typical go-getter is usually a new vice president. The emperor really loves this guy because he's always coming back with the order, the new idea, the breakthrough development. In truth, the go-getter lives off the efforts of others, just like the go-get-her lives off his wife.

He waits for the saleswoman in the field to do all the work with a big customer opportunity, for the chief pro-

=== THE JERKS YOU LEAVE BEHIND ===

grammer to be on the verge of solving a thorny problem, for the market research team to be just about ready to identify a breakthrough trend. Then he jumps in, gets involved himself, takes all the credit.

Go-getters are emperors-in-training. They usually have very short life expectancies themselves and typically last only as long as it takes the emperor to figure out what they're really up to. They want his job. If the emperor waits too long, however, he might get canned himself and replaced by the go-getter.

Go-getters are a resourceful and resilient breed. They're responsible for more than their fair share of firings. No one is safe—emperors or underlings—when there's a real go-getter on the job. Then it's dog eat dog. Odds are it was a go-getter who got you fired in the first place. My own history is littered with them.

· The Sniper ·

Of all the dead men walking, it was the sniper I had the most trouble with. Remember him? The guy who shot down every good idea you ever had? Or stole it for himself if it didn't sound too complicated?

Faulkner had a great line in his trilogy about the Snopes family that applies to all snipers. You know how they call a really great lawyer a "lawyer's lawyer"? And how a really good doctor is a "doctor's doctor"? To paraphrase Faulkner, the sniper is a "son-of-a-bitch's son-of-a-bitch."

These SOBs-squared stand up in every meeting and whine. They didn't get the order because the customer is a flake. The new development project has slipped because the programmers are lazy. The company doesn't have enough support staff. There's never enough money in the budget. It's one excuse after another. I remember one sniper I worked with who thought he was stymied because the company name was all wrong. Did he have any suggestions? Change it, he said.

Some of the more malicious snipers will actually go out of their way to make everyone else look bad. Working together with go-getters, snipers can cost a lot of good people their jobs. They'll kill a project, dry up a sales territory, disembowel a good idea and then blame someone else.

These guys survive because no one dares tell them what everyone really thinks. They're liabilities. Worse than worthless. But no one dares fire them. They're like that really unpleasant kid down the street that no one ever took the time to beat up because it just wasn't worth the aggravation.

· Captain California ·

This is the guy or woman who calls every meeting, copies you on every e-mail he's ever received, is on the road twelve days out of ten, and doesn't have a single unspoken thought. He's a walking, talking, full-length feature movie. An encyclopedia for every buzzword and acronym in the business. He just keeps rolling and rolling. And no one has a clue what he's talking about, let alone what he does.

Captain California has raised elocution to a line item on the balance sheet. Liability, not asset. When he's out in the field, he aggravates customers, suppliers, field staff. He talks his way into more joint ventures and partnering deals than an undeveloped nation. And when he finally takes the time to stay in town long enough to visit the home office, he creates more work for everyone else than a dozen new accounts. He has gills instead of ears. Doesn't listen. Doesn't even stop to breathe.

Even the emperor is intimidated by Captain California. Like the master of disaster, he constantly interrupts the emperor's video golf game. But his job is safe as church. He moves too fast and talks too fast for anyone to catch and fire. A continually moving target. Like a fly that just won't land long enough to whack. All you can do is hope he flies off on his own soon to bug some other poor outfit.

I was blessed to work with Captain California for a brief time several years ago. He lasted three months and created more problems in one weekend than our staff of fifty had in five years.

One Saturday, he dropped by the office to make some quick copies. On his way out, he dumped toner down the toilet, contaminating the landlord's septic system. From there he went to open his vacation home for the season.

At the vacation home, he'd just installed a sump pump and French drains. As he left the house on Sunday, he turned on the furnace to keep the pipes from freezing. The oil pump kicked on, drew oil from the tank that leaked through a break in the feed line caused by installing the French drains. Oil filled the sump. The sump pump kicked on and pumped 250 gallons of oil into the neighbor's yard. The neighbor called the fire department. The fire department called the Environmental Protection Agency. And by first thing Monday morning, Captain California was looking at EPA fines for two contaminations in as many days. He left the company two months later. Thank God.

· The Misfit ·

This is you. The one the emperor yelled at every time he panicked. The one who got burned every time the master of disaster lit another fire. Captain California's favorite audience and the sniper's favorite target. And the one the go-getter just fired because your heart wasn't in it anymore.

I wonder why.

X.

The End?

"... waiting for the telephone to tell me I'm alive ..."
—Counting Crows

All right. I can say what I want to about positve attitude, but until that telephone rings with some kind of opportunity, you're stuck. Right? The world has slapped an embargo on your life, and until you find the key to unlock it, you just have to sit and wait.

It shouldn't be true, but it is. You should be able to take charge of your own life, but you can't. Not really. You can keep getting up every morning, making those calls, following up on those leads, generating ideas. But until someone bites, until that phone rings with a real opportunity, you have nothing.

The waiting game can be long and difficult. I know. But sitting out the race can be good for a while. I remember missing the Boston Marathon a few years ago because of a skiing injury. A blown knee. I was devastated. The injury broke my string of twelve consecutive marathons. But the forced rest gave me the opportunity to do something I hadn't done in a long time: to watch the race instead of run it. And the experience was exhilarating.

Watching the other runners for a change, seeing the spectacle for what it really was, made me want to be a part of it more than ever. The forced rest improved my outlook tremendously. And the following years my enthusiasm for the race was much greater than before.

We are descended from hunter-gatherers, warriors, pioneers, farmers, merchants, and industrialists. Like it or not, we define ourselves through our work. And without work, we may lose track of who we are. Don't let that happen to you. Keep a positive attitude.

Sure, it's hard to go it alone, to keep the ship moving by yourself. There are times when you want to give the wheel to someone else and just take a break. But I hope this book has given you some ideas on how to keep yourself going, to keep up your spirits.

Remember, it's not the end of the line. It's the beginning. Life will measure you on what you do next. So get back on your feet, prepare that résumé, review that financial plan, refresh that contact list, update that log, make those calls, and thank those friends that helped. Then, after a productive morning, reward yourself with an afternoon at the beach, because this is not the worst of times. It's the best.

XI.

Pay Attention to These

May 7

I did it! Just incorporated my new company. Two new partners. Two new computers. Working out of the house, but I'm back in the game. Two big customers on the horizon. And, best of all, people are calling me, looking for work. What a comeback!

It can work for you too. A little patience, perseverence, and listening. It may take some time, but you can pull yourself out of this career crisis. You know you can. Just remember who you are, where you've been, and all the things you've got going for you. If you happen to forget, then remember these:

FIRED WITH ENTHUSIASM

- While it's good to learn from past mistakes, it can be paralyzing trying to focus too much on them now; take a piece of blank paper and write down all the things they said you did wrong at your old job; read through it once, then rip it up and throw it away.

- Assemble all your victories on your résumé: awards, successful projects, big sales; don't embellish, but don't leave any out; make them the foundation of all your future plans.

- Make a list of personal assets; skills, experience, key contacts; match the things you have going for you with the things going against you; now you have the beginnings of a valuable personal planning tool.

- Be proactive; set yourself some realistic goals; start with something simple and reward yourself; don't worry at the end of each day that you didn't do more.

- Stay current; pick a time of day when you're most alert, and read the *Wall Street Journal*, the business section of your local newspaper; follow your industry and its major markets; try to spot ideas, trends, opportunities.

- Get a calendar; fill it up with notes; take your bearings from it every day; keep track of what you do and

PAY ATTENTION TO THESE

what you intend to do; look forward and back and make changes to it often.

- Focus on positive actions; send a card to everyone you know, even the guy who fired you; ask for ideas, advice, and names of people to contact; follow up with a phone call; chances are, they'll want to help.

- Take some time to figure out who you are; make a road map of all the things you've done, successes and failures, victories and defeats; see where it leads you.

- Let go of the old and take control of the new; rearrange the furniture in your house, buy a new outfit, or try a course at night school; get a computer, fax, and e-mail; turn your kitchen into a virtual window on the world.

- Make a detailed financial plan; list everything: savings, severance, unemployment, and part-time income; attack expenses, the mortgage, kids' tuition, and car payments; talk to your creditors and ask them for a break.

- Listen to your kids; don't limit yourself; learn to wish on all the stars.

- Visit friends at other companies to learn new ways of doing things; incorporate what you learn into your own experience and discuss alternatives on interviews.

- Make up a story about yourself that makes you feel comfortable; script a sales pitch, then pick up the telephone and start calling; set yourself a daily goal of three, five, or ten calls; use e-mail and voice mail to increase your effectiveness.

- Make a list of everyone you know and contact them; if someone's hard to reach, try calling before 8:15 A.M.; ask everyone you talk to for two or three more contact names.

- Don't tell them you're looking for a job; ask for advice, ideas; then listen hard, coax them to tell you what they really think; learn to tolerate bad news; and afterward call back just to say thanks.

- Run harder than you think you can run; but avoid fatigue, dress right, and eat from all four food groups.

- Custom fit your résumé to every opportunity; check your list of victories and assets and pick the ones that fit each interview; be brief, get the most from the fewest words.

PAY ATTENTION TO THESE

- Read the prospect company's annual report and its product literature; visit its Web site; figure out how the company is structured, what its goals and expectations are, and how it positions itself relative to its competitors; sell yourself to fit the company's needs.

- Attend free seminars, both in your field and in other fields; learn about new products and trends; make contacts on both sides of the microphone and talk about yourself to everyone.

- Arrive early for interviews and take a short walk, listen to some music, and relax; follow the interviewer's pace, don't rush and don't be rushed; make a list of questions and points about yourself you want to make and refer to it during your interview.

- Wear a suit and tie or nice dress and polished shoes.

- Show them that you've seen it all before; use examples from your old job to fit the new one; borrow from things you've learned on other interviews, from reading product literature, from attending seminars or from visiting other companies.

- Don't be overanxious; be cautious with your follow-up; remember, people are busy, schedules get changed, and nothing happens as fast as you want it to.

FIRED WITH ENTHUSIASM

- Don't be forced to compromise your values; next to your family, your reputation is the most important asset you have; look for the qualities of honesty and integrity in a new boss that you demand in yourself.

- Find out what it takes to be successful at your new company and match your style and personality to the company's; look for personalities that will be stimulating, people who can inspire and lead, leaders who can tell chicken shit from chicken salad.

- Check the company's finances, history, and projections; find out how fast it's taking off and how much runway it has left.

- When starting out, multiply your effectiveness by forming teams; partner with others like yourself to form consulting groups; keep what you earn, but share leads, contacts, and experience.

- When it's time to build a company, consider a virtual corporation; bootstrap your efforts with the free contributions of others; give everyone a share in ownership, but pay no salaries until your product or service generates real revenue.

- When raising money, put lots of sizzle in the front of your business plan: an exciting product, a unique

PAY ATTENTION TO THESE

service, or a breakthrough idea; get the reader's attention right away before he tosses your plan on his growing stack of rejects.

- When you start to hire, look for people who are resourceful, independent, and bring good relationships with them; find someone who can hit a home run first time up at bat, someone who can come right in with a new idea, a key customer, or a major investor in his pocket.

- Beware of success; too much growth can bankrupt, too many customers can stress, too much structure can restrict.

- Consider buying an existing business or a franchise; look for a known name, good references, and a strong order backlog; find something that will pay for itself in three to five years.

- Don't get too high with the highs or too low with the lows.

- Don't let anyone else on the course affect your race.

- Be your own best cheerleader.

- Don't give up when you hit the wall.

Tom Lonergan is an engineer, a former rowing coach, and an entrepreneur who has founded a computer hardware company, a computer software company, and a computer services company. He's led corporate turnarounds, written, lectured, and even holds a carpenter's license. In addition, he's been fired and rehired more times than a baseball manager. He lives in Acton, Massachusetts.